LAMBORGHINI
COUNTACH

Other Titles in the Crowood AutoClassics Series:

LAMBORGHINI COUNTACH
The Complete Story

Peter Dron

CROWOOD
AUTOCLASSICS

First published in 1990 by
The Crowood Press Ltd
Ramsbury, Marlborough
Wiltshire SN8 2HR

Paperback edition 1995

British Library Cataloguing in Publication Data
A catalogue record for this book is available from
the British Library.

ISBN 1 85223 914 X

The photographs in this book were kindly supplied by The Motoring Picture Library, Beaulieu, with the following exceptions: the
photographs on pages 148, 149, 152 (top), 153, 156 and 157 by Mike
Valente are reproduced courtesy of *Car and Driver*. The photographs on pages 24 (top), 59, 60, 80, 81, 87, 88, 89, 92 and 93 were
kindly supplied by Peter Dron. Those on pages 54, 55 (bottom) are
reproduced courtesy of *Fast Lane*; those on pages 56, 117 (top and
middle), 121, 129, 132, 133, 160, 161, 165 by Simon Childs and
those on pages 1, 36 (top) by Rich Newton are also reproduced
courtesy of *Fast Lane*. The photographs on pages 15, 17, 20, 21
(top), 28, 31, 34, 35, 46 (bottom), 91, 122, 123, 169, 172, 180, 183,
184 and 185 were kindly supplied by Lamborghini S.p.A. The
photograph on page 168 is reproduced courtesy of *Motor*. The
photographs on page 76 were kindly supplied by Pirelli. Those on
pages 46 (top), 50, 102, 103 and 150 were kindly supplied by
Prospect Magazines Photo Library. The photograph on page 177 is
reproduced courtesy of Ian Wagstaff.

The line drawings that appear on page 36 (bottom), 90 (top), 111,
115, 125 and 130 were drawn by Nino Acanfora. The line drawings
that appear on pages 38, 44, 45, 98, 99, 126 and 127 were kindly
supplied by Lamborghini S.p.A.

Typeset by Chippendale Type Ltd, Otley, West Yorkshire.
Printed in Great Britain by Butler & Tanner Ltd, Frome and London.

Contents

Acknowledgements

There are several people who deserve thanks for various kinds of help that I have been given.

My greatest thanks must go to my friend Stefano Pasini, who has been a Lamborghini enthusiast for many years. He owns a Silhouette and a Miura SV and is an eye specialist in Bologna. In the gaps which his fourteen-hour working days permit he maintains contact between the factory and Lamborghini clubs throughout the world. He helped to organise the Lamborghini Day referred to in this book, which was a celebration of the first quarter century of Lamborghini cars (at the time of writing, another Lamborghini Day is being organised).

Stefano Pasini is also Editor of *Rivista Lamborghini* ('Lamborghini Review' in English), a magazine published with the official approval of the factory. He says that one of his other tasks is 'to try my best to keep together the Italian owners of Lamborghinis, which is quite a difficult task, strong and hard-headed individualists that they are'. His help in providing background information, particularly on various figures that had proved elusive, was invaluable.

Thanks also to my other good friends at the factory, Sandro Munari, former world-class rally driver, now Lamborghini's test driver and PR man, Marketing Director Ubaldo Sgarzi, a man who's stuck with Lamborghini through good and bad times; Daniele Audetto, who helped me on my first visit to Sant'Agata and who is now Managing Director of Lamborghini Engineering, and responsible for the Lamborghini offshore and Formula 1 engine programmes; and also to Tony Richards, Englishman by birth and American by adoption. He's one of Chrysler's key men at Sant'Agata, and he doesn't take offence if you disagree with him in a vigorous argument. Maybe with him there, Lamborghini will retain some kind of autonomy.

William Jeanes, Editor of *Car and Driver* (circulation nearly one million in a bad month) gave permission for the extracts from various issues of the magazine, likewise John Dinkel, Editor of *Road and Track*; Simon Taylor, Publisher of *Autocar & Motor*; and Ian Fraser, Managing Editor of *Car*.

Finally, I'd like to thank my wife for maintaining her sense of humour most of the time, and for bringing me cups of coffee and other drinks.

Peter Dron
September 1989

Preface

At the time we were creating the Countach, I did not believe that it would be the last car of its type. But then I was producing a new model every two years, and I did not intend to sell the factory.

When I sold it in 1973, it was in fear of the new speed limits (140kph, or 87mph), high taxes on petrol (an increase of 100 per cent) and the prohibition of driving on Saturday and Sunday. Probably if I had stayed, we would have replaced the Countach with another car within a few years.

When we were working on the 4000, we were already studying the possibility of fuel injection. But I did not at that stage consider that there was a need for the five-litre engine. We had been making initially another design for the 4000 four-valve in case some fashion demanded its production. Besides, we had so many orders for the Countach 4000 two-valve that we did not even have the time to think about modifying it.

If I were planning to build a high-performance car today, there is no doubt that I would only build a mid-engined car like the Countach.

F Lamborghini
January 1990

A Brief History of Lamborghini Cars

1963   The first Lamborghini, the 350GTV, appears at the Turin Motor Show, in prototype form.

1964   The 350GT, a tidied-up version of the 350GTV, goes into production.

1965   With the 350GT still in production, Lamborghini displays at Turin the 350GTZ (Zagato) and 350GTS (Spider) show cars.

1966   The 400GT replaces the 350, and the Miura P400 goes into production. A show car, the 400GT Flying Star II, is built.

1967   *Production cars*: Miura 400GT and P400. *Show car*: Marzal.

1968   *Production cars*: Miura 400GT and P400, Islero, Espada. *Show car*: Miura P400 Spider.

1969   *Production cars*: Islero S, Miura P400 (replaced by P400S), Espada.

1970   *Production cars*: Miura P400S, Espada, Jarama. *Show cars*: Jota, Urraco.

1971   *Production cars*: Miura P400S, Miura P400SV, Espada, Jarama. *Show car*: **Countach LP500**.

1972   *Production cars*: Miura P400SV, Espada, Jarama, Urraco P250.

1973   *Production cars*: Espada, Jarama S, Urraco P250, **Countach LP400.**

1974   *Production cars*: Espada, Jarama S, Urraco P250, **Countach LP400.** *Show car*: Bravo.

1975   *Production cars*: Espada, Jarama S, Urraco P250, **Countach LP400.** *Show car*: Urraco competizione.

1976   *Production cars*: Espada, Jarama S, Urraco P250/P200/P300, Silhouette, **Countach LP400.** *Show cars*: Cheetach, Lamborghini/BMW E-26.

1977   *Production cars*: Espada, Jarama S, Urraco P300, Silhouette, **Countach LP400.**

1978   *Production cars*: Espada, Jarama S, **Countach LP400** (replaced by **LP400S**). *Show car*: Espada Frua.

1979   *Production car*: **Countach LP400S.**

1980   *Production car*: **Countach LP400S.**

1981   *Production car*: **Countach LP400S.** *Show car*: Jalpa prototype.

1982   *Production cars*: **Countach LP400S** (replaced by **LP500S**), Jalpa 3500.

1983   *Production cars*: **Countach LP500S**, Jalpa 3500.

1984   *Production cars*: **Countach LP500S**, Jalpa 3500.

1985   *Production cars*: **Countach 5000QV**, Jalpa 3500, LM-002.

1986   *Production cars*: **Countach 5000QV**, Jalpa 3500, LM-002.

1987   *Production cars*: **Countach 5000QV**, Jalpa 3500, LM-002.

1988   *Production cars*: **Countach 5000QV** (replaced by **Countach Anniversary**), Jalpa 3500, LM-002. *Show car*: (from Chrysler USA studios): Portofino.

1989   *Production cars*: **Countach Anniversary**, LM-002.

1990   *Production cars*: **Countach Anniversary** (replaced by **Diablo**), LM-002.

Right: *This late-model 5000* quattrovalvole *has the side skirts and front bib spoiler which foreshadowed the more extensive alterations of the Anniversary model.*

Introduction

To most people, even to many car enthusiasts, the Lamborghini Countach is an absurdity. Nobody *needs* the best part of 500bhp in a road car, and nobody who likes to travel with more than a toothbrush and a change of underwear would consider the Countach 'practical': it is only 42in (1,067mm) high, has a weird door mechanism, and simply getting in and out of it calls for litheness if not athleticism. Once you've squeezed in, there isn't much space, even compared with other two-seaters, but externally, the car is abnormally wide. The boot, on the other hand, is ludicrously small. Visibility is appalling, even without the vulgar and unnecessary rear wing, which most sensible purchasers delete from the list of desirable options. The prescribed method of reversing is for the driver to sit on the sill and look back across the roof.

Starting the engine demands a degree of skill and sensitivity, and different techniques are required depending upon whether the engine is being fired up from cold or after a long run. Stalling in traffic is unlikely, except as a result of incompetence (or failed muscle in the leg that operates the clutch pedal) but the Countach does not enjoy being chugged around in the rush hour. Nor will its occupants. It is inadvisable to use a Countach in bad weather, as its big tyres cannot cope with snow and ice and there is a serious danger of aquaplaning in heavy rain.

A potentially strong rival to Ferrari's 308/328, Lamborghini's 'entry-level' model, the Jalpa, was let down mainly by its chunky appearance.

The Jalpa's mid-mounted 3.5-litre V8 produced 235bhp (and a glorious sound), giving a top speed of almost 150mph (241kph). The replacement model, the P140 Bravo, is to be powered by a V10 engine.

On top of all this, it costs a vast amount of money; the servicing bills are simply horrifying, and the insurance companies will laugh if you ask which group it falls into.

Yet the paradox is that it is these very qualities which contribute to the Countach's success. Its logic is its lack of logic: if you have so much money that money is no object and you want a wild toy – this argument runs – then you might as well get yourself the wildest toy in the world.

In the summer of 1986, I visited Sant' Agata as an infidel. I'd never driven a Countach, and not only didn't believe the 5000QV would do the kinds of speeds that they said it would do, but somehow doubted its engineering integrity. I didn't really have anything solid on which to base this view,

but when you're prejudiced against something, who needs evidence? I had an image of Lamborghini as a bunch of dilettanti operating out of a run-down factory. If this impression had ever been accurate, it was several years out of date. What I found was a group of dedicated, concerned managers, trying desperately to keep the company moving forward; a workforce with the kind of craft-skills I had previously seen in few places (such as Aston Martin) and who – most surprisingly – seemed to work with great dedication and pride. What I found, above all, was a product which was worthy of this hard work.

I had driven a Jalpa. Much to my surprise, and despite a few flaws, I found it was rather a good car. The V8 engine in particular was

This rear view shows how helpful the rear wing is to rearward vision, and also how the ungainly add-on rear panel (this is a 1989 US-specification 5000QV) destroys the trapezoidal tail-light clusters. The twin 'power bulges' in the engine cover are for the fuel injection.

fabulous – the sound it made was very similar to that of a Cosworth DFV Grand Prix engine. The chassis was quite good and felt that with a bit of investment in development engineering, it could possibly be better than Ferrari's 308/328.

I was amazed by my first drive in a Countach, however. The chassis was so responsive, the brakes so powerful, the steering so accurate – in short the car was well engineered; but that engine! Words cannot describe the sound that Lamborghini's 5.2 litre V12 makes as it approaches 8,000rpm in fifth gear. It is simply staggering.

It could be argued that Lamborghini invented the modern supercar with the Countach's predecessor, the Miura, but it was the Countach which took the concept to its logical extreme.

Now that Ferrari have replaced the 328 with the technically-superior but rather tubby-looking 348, Lamborghini have an opportunity to seize the advantage. The investment money is there now to do it properly this time, and make up for the failures of the Urraco and Jalpa to live up to expectations.

I hope I have done justice to the Countach's long and tangled history. It has been a fascinating experience.

Right: *Apart from its smaller wheels and tyres, this 1984 5000S is externally indentical to the later quattrovalvole, though substantially slower.*

1 The Philosophy Which Made the Countach

The 'philosophy' behind the Countach was not based on modern marketing principles. Its design was not derived from detailed and expensive research into what the 'target' customer wanted from such a car. There were no 'customer clinics' (apart from the Geneva Show) in which people could compare the new Lamborghini directly with its rivals. Instead, with appealing Italian arrogance, it was the creation of a small group of single-minded men of enormous talent who asked *themselves*, rather than anyone else, the question: what is it that *I* want from a high-performance car?

What they wanted was an extremely powerful engine, with chassis behaviour to match. For example, they didn't feel the need for more than a minimum of comfort. They didn't want electrically-operated windows, a radio/cassette player (and they wouldn't have wanted a mobile compact-disc player or a mobile phone if such fancy gizmos had then been available), air-conditioning, or central locking. In the simplest terms, all they wanted was the best toy you could have for use on the public highway; that's the way Lamborghini designed it, and that's the way the Countach was built.

Thus the Countach was right from the beginning what could be termed a purist's car, in other words it was a racing car for road use; it was the definitive modern supercar.

STRIKING OUT

From the beginning, Lamborghini was not trying to imitate Ferrari, or any other competitor, but to strike out on a different path. The story that, snubbed by Enzo Ferrari, Ferruccio Lamborghini had stormed away, resolved to get a kind of revenge by building a better car is one of the colourful myths surrounding this colourful man. He has never taken the trouble to deny it; but the simpler truth appears to be that he was an Italian industrialist and engineer with a passion for fast cars – having owned several, including some Ferraris – and he was, in the early 1960s, a wealthy man.

It is not uncommon for the more flamboyant type of successful industrialist to want to become a sports car manufacturer. Many of them believe that they can make sustained profits out of such an exciting business; a few succeed.

Lamborghini Cars was an established manufacturer well before the Countach appeared on the drawing boards. There was even less reason for the Miura's replacement to imitate anything else. Quite the opposite was true, in fact: the charging bull symbol had now become established as a by-word for the cutting edge of modern technology, and it was almost imperative that the new car should be more extreme than anything else the factory had previously produced.

Lamborghini did not need to follow the

Ferruccio Lamborghini, practical engineer, tractor manufacturer, industrialist, and creator of a line of remarkable high-performance cars. His last connection with the car factory was severed in 1974, and today he is a successful wine producer.

Ferruccio Lamborghini

Born on 28 April 1916 (which makes him a Taurus), at Renazzo di Cento, a small village fifteen miles north of Bologna, Ferruccio Lamborghini came from a simple farming family. From an early age, he was interested in mechanical engineering, and after studying for an industrial arts degree in Bologna, he became an apprentice in an engineering shop.

During World War II, he was stationed on the island of Rhodes, which fell to the British in 1944. It is not clear whether or not he became a prisoner of war. In 1946 he was able to return home to Renazzo di Cento.

Responding to local demand, he began to build tractors from scrap materials. By 1949 this had expanded into a thriving business and had made his fortune. Production figures rose from one tractor per day to 1,500 per year by 1958, and to 5,000 per year in 1969. With an unusually high proportion of components made 'in-house', the tractors had a good reputation for reliability.

By 1960 he had expanded his business empire to include a factory making heating and air-conditioning equipment for domestic and industrial premises. Four years later he became a car manufacturer, and the long and occasionally tortured history of Automobili Lamborghini S.p.A. began. Lamborghini sold his tractor company in 1972, a year after moving into larger premises.

In 1974 his last links with the car factory were severed. He now produces wines (red, white and rosé) from his vineyards at Panicarola, Perugia. The label on the bottles includes a shield depicting the rampant bull. Like his cars and his tractors, the Lamborghini wines are known for their high quality.

Ferruccio Lamborghini was not the first, nor the last, wealthy, creative industrialist to have believed he could increase his fortune (or at least have fun while not going bankrupt) by building sports cars.

Ferrari path, which was moving gradually, even then, towards practicality at the expense of raw excitement. Lamborghini, though the management of the company did not always understand the point clearly enough, was all about raw excitement tempered only by engineering of the finest quality.

It is interesting, though, to consider the Countach in this sense: as the true successor to the muscular (some might say truck-like) Daytona. Whereas the Boxer, and even more so, its replacement, the Testarossa, were designed with a great deal of attention to

More than the Berlinetta Boxer and Testarossa, which are essentially 'soft' cars, the Countach was the spiritual successor to the Ferrari 365 Daytona, shown here in rare (genuine) cabriolet form.

refinement, ride quality and general ease of use, the Countach was always far less compromised.

That is not to suggest that it was designed deliberately to be uncomfortable, noisy and impractical. In fact, it is not that uncomfortable (especially in later versions, with increased headroom); anyone who describes the sound of a Lamborghini V12 as 'a noise' is a philistine, and as for practicality, it depends upon your definition of the word. It is rather that a different set of priorities was in operation. It must be remembered that Lamborghini was aiming at a far smaller sector of the market even than Ferrari, where they never produce more than 4,500 cars a year as a matter of principle, and in the face of fierce demand from all over the world. (It might be interjected here that you can afford principles more easily when you're owned by Fiat, as Ferrari already was

at that time. Let us hope that Lamborghini's relationship with Chrysler is at least as good.)

Alejandro de Tomaso – having bought Maserati – once boasted that he had built more cars the year before than Ferrari. When I mentioned this to a contact at Ferrari, he merely smiled, and said: 'OK, but how much profit does he make?' Here we have two different perceptions of what is important in business. De Tomaso's remark is symptomatic of the motor industry's obsession with numbers, whereas the Ferrari man's response indicates a more intelligent approach. It may actually seem obvious, but it is remarkable how many companies (even specialist ones) fail to understand it: some – large and small – have gone bankrupt in pursuit of a higher market share.

There was no chance of Countach production ever flooding the market. Its makers

*A brand-new factory for a brand-new make of car: journalists at
the official opening of the Sant'Agata plant in 1964.*

Perhaps not as elegant as some of the rival Italian sports coupes of the time, the 350GT with its 3.5-litre V12 engine was nevertheless an exciting and well-engineered car, the foundation of the factory's reputation.

Chassis

What are the advantages of having the engine centrally mounted, and more especially with the gearbox actually ahead of the engine? The *disadvantages* are obvious, because the cabin size and luggage capacity are instantly harmed. (Never mind the advantages in marketing hype. That is a subject for a different kind of book.)

The dynamic reasons for placing the engine between the driver and the back axle, convincingly demonstrated on race tracks over the past thirty years, are connected mainly with achieving a low polar moment of inertia, but also – at least potentially – with aerodynamic advantages, because of the possibility of having a lower nose section.

When, as in racing cars and in the Countach, the radiators are also placed centrally rather than in the front of the car, this advantage is increased, and it also leads to a smoother profile: so there is a potential improvement in efficiency as well as in stability, two aspects of aerodynamics which do not always march forward hand in hand.

But is a low polar moment of inertia desirable in a road car? The theoretical advantage in handling is that with the majority of its weight concentrated near its centre, a mid-engined car responds more rapidly to control inputs. This is of positive benefit in a racing car, where cornering is constantly close to the roadholding limits in known bends. The mid-engined car is actually less stable around its own vertical axis. Think of a dumbell pivoted at its centre. With the weights at each end, it takes greater effort to make the dumbell turn than when the weights are moved towards the centre. Thus, the mid-engined car turns into corners more readily than a front-engined or rear-engined car.

That is all very well on a racing circuit, where the bends are well known. But in road driving, one is often faced with tightening radii and varying camber, and having the ultimate cornering machine is not necessarily an advantage. It is actually more difficult to control and, especially for a road car, the classic front-engine/rear-drive solution, makes for greater ease of control because the response rate is more gradual.

For a skilled driver, it can actually be useful to have a car which changes direction easily, and whose inherent characteristic is not necessarily ultimate stability. At the other end of the scale, the average driver probably needs his message of slip angle leading to slide at an early rather than a late stage in the bend. At least, then, the accident may occur at lower speed. And even the skilled driver will find more gradual responses an advantage on unknown roads, unless – like a rally driver – he knows there is nothing coming the other way and can put a degree of directional instability to his advantage.

To the extent that the car which stands most obviously at the opposite end of the spectrum from the Countach in this respect – the Porsche 911 (especially in Turbo form), in which the engine overhangs the rear axle – is universally regarded as a 'difficult' car to drive, you might think the case proven. But this is all theory. Porsche has developed several of its 911s to handle very well indeed, be it on race tracks, in rallies, or for road driving. And there is still nothing wrong with the front-engine/rear-drive configuration.

In fact, although the placing of masses within the chassis clearly has a significant effect on the handling of a car, just as important is the development engineer's work in choosing and developing the best possible suspension design, steering, brakes and (perhaps above all) the best size and construction of tyre.

In any case, why should anyone who has bought a Countach to *drive* it be worried about such considerations? He will have, as well as plenty of money, some inherent skill which has been honed as far as possible by experience and instruction. Let us hope so. . .

Besides that, a Countach has such high cornering power that its driver is likely to be intimidated while still in an area of behaviour which could be described as 'grip' rather than 'handling.'

were not interested in building more cars than Ferrari or anyone else, only in building better ones.

The Countach in some ways also represented Ferruccio Lamborghini's last, defiant gesture. By the time he gave it his final blessing, he already had one foot outside the door, so perhaps some might consider that he was not so brave in committing the company to an adventure for which he would not personally bear the possible consequences.

But that would be unfair. In its time, the Miura had perhaps been an even greater gamble, which Ferruccio had taken at a time when his companies seemed relatively secure. Bizarre as it may have been, the Countach was no more than a logical development of the Miura, designed to look even more dramatic, to be even faster, to attract wealthy customers. Quite simply, it

was a sound and sensible business decision to put the Countach into production, even if it is unlikely (with the wisdom of hindsight) that such a step would have been taken a year or two afterwards, when the 'oil crisis' was in full flow. But by then, it was too late.

Also, it must be borne in mind that the creation of the Countach took on – as such projects often do (especially when the boss's mind is preoccupied) – a momentum of its own. The Miura, for example, though a team effort, was basically engineered by Dallara. It had been a great car, an image-maker, and it had forced Ferrari to reconsider the direction its cars should take in the future. When Dallara departed, the Countach was a chance for Paolo Stanzani to make a name for himself by once more re-defining the concept of the supercar.

In 1965, Touring of Milan (creators of 'Superleggera' bodywork) produced two of these 350GT 'Spider' dropheads.

Ing Giampaolo Dallara (wearing spectacles) is seen here at the first showing of the 400GT, a 2 + 2 which was a more practical road car than its predecessor. It was fitted with a bored-out 3.9-litre version of the V12.

TAMING THE BULL

When Dave McLellan, Chief Project Engineer of the Corvette, speaks of his approach to chassis design, particularly in relation to the ZR–1, he refers disparagingly to some other high-performance cars, in which the driver is forced to make huge efforts and to concentrate intensely in order to avoid making even minor errors, and then even greater efforts to correct them when he has committed them. He uses the expression, 'Taming the bull'.

Right: Lamborghini's 'charging bull' badge was not only a humorous response to the prancing horse of Maranello, but a suitably powerful image for a powerful breed of cars.

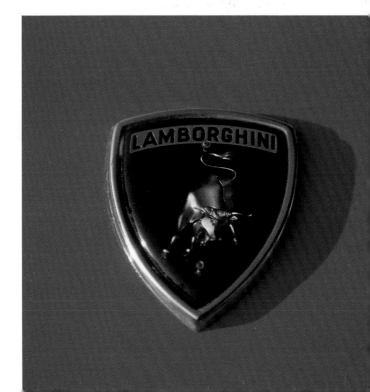

Although this is not intended as a direct reference to Lamborghini, it may be considered appropriate, at least by those who have never driven a Countach (which is, of course, the overwhelming majority of the world's population – and even, it might be worth adding, the overwhelming majority of the relatively few people in the world who could afford to buy one). But in fact the Countach is considerably more 'user-friendly' than might be imagined.

There is, of course, almost a disdain of practicality about the car. It is difficult to get into, even, because the door opening is small, and the car is so very low. It is comfortable enough once you've learnt the prescribed method of crawling into it – or at least it is if you are of typical Italian dimensions. Someone of my height (nearly 6ft 4in) is never going to be really comfortable in a Countach. But it's not like trying to squeeze into a Caterham 7. There is plenty of room for a tall person to operate the pedals of the Countach, and (just) to turn the steering wheel fully without banging the knees.

The door opening system in the Countach is of course still more ridiculous – adding unnecessary weight, complicating the manufacturing process (thereby increasing the cost) and making the task of getting in and out of the car difficult even for the young and fit. Then there is the question of escape in a rollover. Apparently the prescribed method is to kick out the windscreen, though that would only work in some circumstances.

The only person I know who has ever been in a position (upside-down in a field) in which such action was necessary is Lamborghini's chief tester Valentino Balboni, an apparently fearless but highly skilled driver, who unsuccessfully attempted to avoid a heavy lorry which emerged from a side road when he was testing a customer's Countach S.

The last of the Countaches, the Anniversary, is the most comfortable of all, though I am not at all sure that I approve of the adoption of electric seat adjustment and electric windows – if you can call those postbox-sized slots 'windows': they are useless even for the task for which they are designed – making a payment at one of Italy's numerous and ludicrous autostrada tolls, where you can queue for ten minutes in order to pay a fee equivalent to thirty pence.

But anyone who criticises the Countach for its lack of practicality is being absurd. The Countach is, people say, an outdated concept, so here is an outdated, sexist remark: if a man marries a beautiful woman mainly because he expects his socks to be washed, it is more than likely that he will be unhappy.

THE DEFINITIVE SUPERCAR

It must be remembered that when the idea of the Countach was conceived, there was considerably less traffic in Europe than is the case today. Above all, there was still a distinction, even if it was already blurring at the edges, between what was expected of a 'sports car' and of a saloon car. The Golf GTi had not yet arrived, to make a nonsense of cars like the MGB.

It is also mistaken to suggest that the Countach is designed only for being driven at exceptionally high speeds on the *autostrada*. It is true that I wince whenever I see one with two wheels up on the kerb in the West End of London, but a well-driven Countach can give a very good account of itself on twisting roads.

Its main drawback in this respect has nothing to do with dynamics, but everything to do with dimensions: although to a large extent you can forget about the appalling rear and rear three-quarter visibility once you are on the move, you can never forget the car's width. Any driver with the slightest

Well engineered counter-balancing makes operation of the
'paper-cutter' doors simple enough, though they do not leave
very large apertures for the Countach's occupants.

Left: *The author (right) and Stefano Pasini examine the unique 350GTV show car at Emilianauto in Bologna. This was the original show car – the very first Lamborghini not designed for use on a farm – which evolved into the 350GT. Since this photograph was taken in 1986, this interesting relic has been painstakingly restored.*

Below: *As is the case with Ferraris, the best colour for a Countach is red, though the car also looks intriguingly aggressive in black.*

Compare this rear view of the European-spec 5000QV with the American version shown in the Introduction. This (apart from the wing) is what the car is supposed to look like.

imagination will feel somewhat intimidated by this, particularly when driving on narrow roads with blind bends. I'm not considering single-track lanes here, but rather the kind of English roads in which there is enough space for two cars travelling in opposite directions to pass without the need for braking, or for closing one eye and hoping.

This is generally true of the majority of cars of very high performance, the most notable exception being the Porsche 911 whose narrowness is an important component of its ability to move from one place to another in a very short time. On the other hand, if it is possible to see through most of the corners in a stretch of road, the Countach can see off almost anything . . .

It is undeniable that the car feels most in its element when the engine can be wound towards the rev limit in the upper two gears. It's one of those cars which come into their own at speeds which are illegal in most countries. The Ferrari Daytona was another, only more so. At less than 100mph (161kph), the Countach does not feel like a lorry, but one is more aware of a certain heaviness in all the controls, especially the steering, clutch and brakes. Above that speed, it loosens up nicely, and feels precise rather than ponderous.

It is indeed true that on a wet, twisting road, a skilled driver of a GTi can get away from a Countach, especially in Italy where they dislike the concept of rain and accordingly refuse to build a crown into most of their roads; the result is that as soon as it rains, there is a layer of water for practice in aquaplaning, and when you have 345/35 section rear tyres – even, as these are, very good tyres, and never mind the fact that the traction of the car is outstanding – you will experience aquaplaning in these circumstances. The front tyres will begin the process, and by the time the rears lift themselves on

to the cushion of water, you are already 9½ parts out of 10 out of control.

The sensible answer to this is not to take your Countach out if you expect bad weather, and to drive it gently if you get caught in a storm. And no, I don't accept that that makes a nonsense of the car.

In support of this, Paul Frère, the celebrated journalist and former racing driver has made the observation about the Countach that:

'The only excuse for the virtually non-existent rear view and completely non-existent rear three-quarter visibility is that it is fast enough to make the possibility of anyone coming up behind very unlikely – that is, if you are competent enough to drive it as it should be driven. As far as practicality is concerned, a lot could be written, but this almost absurd concentration on speed is probably why people buy a Countach. When I say "people", I mean "men" for, from every point of view, this is really a man's car, if only for the effort required by the clutch, the gearchange, or the steering. Neither do I think that women are unreasonable enough to get involved in a love affair with such a beast – and buying a Countach can only be a love affair.'

Despite all its oddities, and despite the factory's industrial problems, despite the oil crisis, against all the odds, the Countach emerged as a remarkable production car. There have been numerous imitators, and it is certain that the Countach had a marked effect on Ferrari, if only to force the longer-established manufacturer to take a significantly different direction with the Testarossa, and then to admit – by the creation of the GTO and F40 – that it needed a ferociously fast car for 'image' purposes.

The Countach set new yardsticks. It was the definitive supercar.

2 Defining the Definitive

Today, Lamborghini is about to find out whether it's got the right answer to the question: 'What sort of cars should we build for the 1990s?' In retrospect, the question of what sort of car should Lamborghini have built for the 1970s seems obvious: the Countach. It's always easier to answer questions in retrospect . . .

In 1969, Lamborghini was at a peak of its success as a car manufacturer: the Miura S had established the company as a producer of innovative sports cars, brilliantly designed and engineered and the four-seater Espada (of which 1,217 were produced) was also in high demand.

Two difficulties had to be surmounted. First, to provide volume, Lamborghini wanted to build a car which would fulfil the role of Porsche's 911. The Urraco appeared in prototype form at the 1970 Turin Show, with a good pedigree (engineering by Stanzani, styling by Bertone), but it never achieved the desired success, suffering too many problems. Second, at the other end of the scale, the Miura was almost *too* successful: Lamborghini needed to be seen to be more exclusive than Ferrari, and the Miura was no longer a rare sight among those who could afford such cars. To many people, 'rarity value' is often more important than engineering excellence and sheer beauty. To those who could spot the difference, anyway, the Miura's chassis was some way short of perfection: this technically fascinating car was rather unstable at the top end of its high speed capability.

Elsewhere, plenty of mid-engined cars were beginning to appear to rival the Miura: the eccentric Argentine Alejandro de Tomaso, down the road in Modena, created the Mangusta (beautiful though not *very* fast and also quite a handful) and the Pantera (a strange Italian/American mulatto which, though ergonomically appalling, performed impressively and – against all the odds – was to enjoy one of the longest production runs of any sports car in history). The Maserati Bora (among the last *real* Maseratis) appeared in 1971 and in the same year Lamborghini's fiercest rival, Ferrari, replaced the beautiful, extremely fast but very old-fashioned Daytona with the 365BB (Berlinetta Boxer).

So it was almost inevitable that Lamborghini had to move towards a car more extreme, faster, more advanced technically, and more dramatic aesthetically than either the Miura or the supercars built by rival firms.

THE COUNTACH EMERGES

Not the least extraordinary aspect of the Countach was the short period of time following initial concept discussions between Ferruccio Lamborghini and Paolo Stanzani and the completion of the first running prototype (Dallara had already left by this time). The first functional prototype was almost complete in 1971. Perhaps because the car displayed at the Geneva Show of that year was not fully ready as a road car, some

The 'SV' was the last and best version of the Miura. This one is shown outside the factory awaiting delivery.

observers believed the Countach had been conceived merely as a show car. But this was not so: it was designed from the outset to replace the Miura. Even so, rejection of the prototype by journalists and the public could well have knocked the entire project on the head. But as it turned out, the Geneva Show stand, with the Miura SV and the Countach alongside one another, was an enormous success. So many orders were placed for the Countach that it was obvious that it would have to enter production as soon as practically possible.

The Countach began its life under the drab title of 'Project 112', a designation which survived into the chassis numbering system. The show car was described as the 'LP500' (which stood for 'Longitudinale Posteriore Cinque Litri', which is more or less self-explanatory). But why was it called 'Countach'?

The word itself has origins in the local Torinese dialect, and a rough translation into English is 'Wow! Look at that!' There are several explanations of how it came to be applied to this Lamborghini. The most plausible is that Nuccio Bertone used it in the presence of Ferruccio Lamborghini when Gandini's proposal was unveiled for the first time.

Giampaolo Dallara

Born in 1939, Dallara came from a wealthy background (his father, the mayor of a mountain village, built his own private race track, which was later used for testing Lamborghinis). He had a degree in aeronautical engineering from the Technical Institute of Milan and was only twenty-four when he joined Lamborghini in March 1962 as Chief Engineer. He had previously worked as an engineer at Ferrari (thanks to one of his professors, who worked there part-time) and then with his cousin Giulio Alfieri (later to be Lamborghini's Chief Engineer) at Maserati.

Although he left Lamborghini to pursue his motor racing interests in 1968, before the creation of the Countach, he played an important role in laying the foundations for it. With Stanzani and Wallace, Dallara engineered the Miura. In designing it, he drew inspiration from the Le Mans-winning Ford GT40.

In the difficult years of the late 1970s, Dallara worked as an occasional consultant for the company, enticed back by the Canadian industrialist Walter Wolf, whom some thought at the time might take over the factory, so he had some influence on the later development of the Countach. He is rated by many as one of the best road-car chassis engineers of modern times, and was one of those most responsible for establishing Lamborghini's reputation as a considerable manufacturer of high-performance road cars. However, it seems that Stanzani, originally his assistant, is a better development engineer.

Paolo Stanzani

Born in Bologna a year earlier than Dallara, and into a less wealthy family, Stanzani left Maserati to join Lamborghini at the same time, where he was initially factory manager. In 1968, he succeeded Dallara as Chief Engineer. Stanzani and his assistant, test engineer Massimo Parenti, and chief tester Bob Wallace methodically removed the flaws from Dallara's inspired Miura. They eventually brought it to the peak of its development in the form of the SV, in 1971.

After that he was fully responsible for the engineering of the Countach. In particular, the ingenious drivetrain arrangement, with the gearbox ahead of the engine and connected to the differential by means of a shaft running rearwards inside the engine crankcase, was his.

He left Lamborghini in 1975, when it seemed unlikely that Lamborghini had a future. He is now the engineering brains behind the re-born Bugatti company. Almost entirely because of his presence there, the Bugatti project is rated as more likely to succeed than the Cizeta.

DESIGN AND DEVELOPMENT

Technically, the Miura had been interesting in having a transversely-mounted V12. Although its shape was possibly inspired by the Le Mans-winning Ford GT40s, it was therefore very different under the skin. The transverse mounting had been selected for sound reasons (such as economical use of space), though the challenge and marketing value of being different from everyone else must have been at least another significant factor.

It was evident from the outset that the Miura's successor would be mid-engined, but the blank sheet of paper in Stanzani's hands

It is improbable that anyone will ever devise a cleaner shape for
a closed sports coupe than the Miura, created by Marcello
Gandini when he was Bertone's chief designer.

Fine lines, subtle curves and distinctive grille features are all trademarks of Gandini.

after Dallara's departure gave Stanzani the chance to reconsider the approach to this configuration. His chassis took the low-polar-movement approach farther than any previous road car, although by now he appreciated more fully the virtues of a more conventional mounting of the engine, as used in most racing cars, then and now – still between the seats and the back axle, but with the crankshaft in-line with the longitudinal axis.

This is a better solution for numerous, fairly obvious reasons: it is much easier to devise an efficient exhaust system for it, cooling presents fewer difficulties, there is a reduction in cabin noise (the Miura was *very*

loud), and servicing becomes far simpler. But above all, a 'north-south' location improves the weight distribution, and Stanzani had realised how vital a component this was of handling stability.

The engine he planned to use was the familiar V12, but with the displacement (or capacity) increased to 4,971cc. However, there were serious development problems, and it was not until considerably later that an engine of approximately that size was used successfully, so really there is a strong case for calling the first prototype an LP400, since the 'LP500' existed only in the imagination.

The crucial question was where to place

Above and right: *This is the Lamborghini-engined version of the Bizzarrini P538, built in 1967 (two others were made, but with Corvette V8s). It was an indication of the direction which Giotto Bizzarrini wanted to take when he designed the engine in 1963, but Ferruccio Lamborghini did not wish to be involved in racing.*

At the launch of the Miura in 1967, two British visitors look on: the late Colin Chapman (described by the Italian caption writer as 'David Niven'!) with Jim Clark, who was killed in the following year. Factory tester Bob Wallace can just be seen behind Clark, while the man on the right with the white shirt is Ferruccio Lamborghini.

Inside the Sant'Agata factory, with Miura production in full swing. The V12 engines in the foreground are for the Miura, those further away (with side-mounted air filter boxes and in-line gearboxes) are for the front-engined cars.

*This photograph shows the compactness of the Miura's engine/
transmission: it was ingeniously engineered, but sharing of
lubricant was less than ideal.*

the five-speed gearbox, and it was here that
Stanzani applied a master stroke. With the
weight distribution his main consideration,
he decided to attach it to the front ('north'
end) of the engine. A further advantage of
this, of course, was that it eliminated the
need for a long and complex gear linkage,
which can lead to poor gearchange quality.
However, some ingenious engineering was
necessary to make such a location possible.
A shaft passed back through the crankcase
to the differential, which increased manufacturing complexity (and hence cost) but
which was reckoned to give more advantages than drawbacks.

Even though it required extensive development, this was undoubtedly better than the
solution employed in the original Miura in
which (as in the BMC Mini) the same oil was
used to lubricate both engine and gearbox:
that may be all right for a low-cost production car (though few engineers agreed with
the late Sir Alex Issigonis on that point) but
was very much short of ideal in a high-
quality high-performance car. The final –
and by far the best – version of the Miura,
the SV, had separate lubrication for its
engine and gearbox.

Although by this time many racing chassis
were of monocoque construction, Stanzani
chose to use a spaceframe for the Countach.
The prototype's chassis had been relatively
simple, with square-section tubing, but in
the final production version, thin, round-
section tubes were used. This chassis was
considerably more intricate and complex

Tight fit: LP5000S engine in the 1981 Countach. Mounting the carburettors horizontally put rearward vision higher up the list of priorities than engine breathing, positions which were reversed in the quattrovalvole.

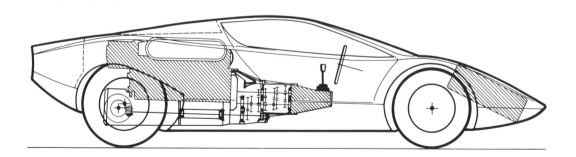

This diagram shows clearly the ingenious mechanical layout of the Countach, with the drive from the engine passing forwards to the gearbox, and thence rearwards via an enclosed shaft in the sump to the differential. The penalty of this arrangement is that the engine is raised by a few inches.

than that of the Maserati Tipo 61 of 1959, which became known as the 'Birdcage'. Stanzani's reason for this decision was the pursuit of lightness and rigidity. Stanzani and Gandini also planned to shape the chassis in such a way that its outer surfaces would act as supports for the body panels, taking a step further the system patented by the Touring coachwork company, whose *Superleggera* design had been successfully used on a number of cars including Aston Martins.

Those who today criticise the work of Marcello Gandini should examine the purity of line of his original Countach 'LP500'. Its essential feature, and the chief contributory factor to the car's striking appearance, is a single, curving line, running rearwards at right angles to the thin slot across the front of the car, over the windscreen and back to the characteristically hexagonal tail-lamp cluster. All other curves, lines and angles are subsidiary to this single, boldly sweeping stroke. This is without doubt the touch of a master, the type of feature which is often imitated in the work of talented design students, but which can only rarely be transferred successfully from flat-work into a three dimensional reality.

Marcello Gandini is a purist and an individualist. It is therefore not surprising that he has difficulty in dealing with marketing men. He abhors anything in his designs which does not perform an essential function. Thus that first Countach design, though elegant, was complex and created plenty of engineering difficulties: the Countach was designed to have a minimum number and size of air intakes, and to have all areas of the body as flush as possible to the overall shape.

It was as well that Bob Wallace, the company's Chief Tester, was around to identify simple, practical problems (the most obvious of which in the early stages of testing was lack of air to the radiators) and to seek solutions for them. But a rear 'wing'

Marcello Gandini

Born in Turin in 1938, Marcello Gandini is one of the world's greatest car designers.

From an early age, he was interested in design, and his first automotive work was as a consultant for Abarth in the early 1960s. In 1965 he replaced Giugiaro as Bertone's chief designer; he stayed with Bertone for fourteen years, during which he was responsible for a number of dramatic road cars, especially for Lamborghini, including the Miura (1966), Espada (1968), Jarama (1970), Urraco (1971) and Countach (1972). Other sports cars include the Iso Lele (1969), Maserati Khamsin (1972), Fiat X1/9 and Ferrari Dino GT4 (1973), and – perhaps his masterpiece – the Lancia Stratos of 1974.

But he also designed more conventional cars, such as the BMW 2500 (1969) and 520 (1972), VW Polo (1975) and Alfa Romeo Alfetta 2000 (1977). In 1979 he left Bertone, having already designed the Citroen BX (which appeared in 1983), to sign a five-year exclusive contract with Renault. This led to the Renault Superfive and the interiors of the GTA and 25.

His most recent (and perhaps most controversial) work is the Cizeta V16-T, and the similarities and differences between that and the new Lamborghini Diablo (and the background story behind the creation of the two cars) are almost worthy of a book on their own.

---

did not find a place in Gandini's imagination.

If that first design lacks some of the 'macho', brutal appeal of the later Countaches (at its peak in the 5000QV, before being compromised as the uncomfortable-looking Anniversary model), it nevertheless provided the genetic fingerprint for all the car's subsequent developments.

One of the hallmarks of the Countach's design, and which set it apart from anything that had previously appeared, was its door-

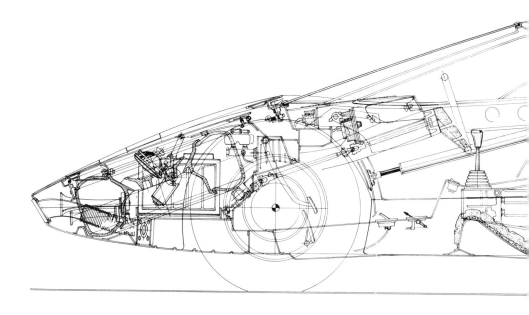

This is the original engineering side elevation for the LP500, the first of the Countaches. At this stage the intention was to run a single distributor off one of the four camshafts.

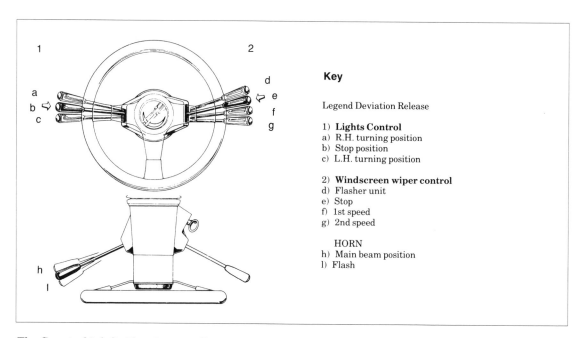

Key

Legend Deviation Release

1) **Lights Control**
a) R.H. turning position
b) Stop position
c) L.H. turning position

2) **Windscreen wiper control**
d) Flasher unit
e) Stop
f) 1st speed
g) 2nd speed

   HORN
h) Main beam position
l) Flash

The Countach's left-side column stalk operates the indicators, headlights main beam/flash and horn, while that on the right operates the two-speed windscreen wiper.

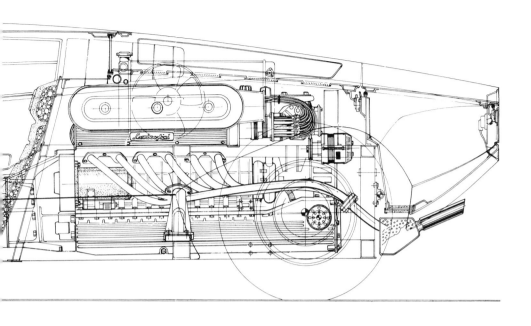

*The Countach that never was – except as a show car. The purity
of Gandini's original design is shown in this side view of the
LP500. Note that the rear wheelarch design is repeated almost
exactly in today's Diablo.*

Starting up a Countach

Because of its row of six guzzling twin-choke carburettors, firing up a Countach requires the application of a particular technique; or rather, of *two* particular techniques, since a different approach must be used depending upon the heat of the engine. Here is what the handbook recommends (though it must be remembered that this is only a rough guide, since each engine differs very slightly from any other). So there is art here as well as technique:

'The control must be set as follows:
   Gear lever in neutral.
   Depress clutch pedal to eliminate gearbox passive resistance and to ease starting.
   Turn the ignition key clockwise to the first "click". Wait until the two electric pumps have charged the starting circuit with pressure.
   Since the engine does not require a special device for starting (choke), simply press the accelerator pedal three or four times. This has the desired effect of enriching the fuel mixture.
   Now turn the ignition key clockwise again to activate the starter motor. As soon as the engine has started, release the key, it will return automatically to its prior position. If the engine has not started, return the key to its initial position, and repeat the procedure.
   When the engine is started cold, accelerate gradually and do not exceed 3,000–4,000rpm, so as to enable oil in sufficient quantities to reach those points that require lubrication.
   Furthermore, do not accelerate flat-out until the water temperature has reached 70°C.'

There is no mention anywhere of the popping and banging as the engine picks up on five cylinders, and then three entirely different ones, and then seven, all the while threatening to stall.
   But in my experience, starting an engine like this from cold is altogether easier than firing it up when you've given it a good long run and then parked it for a couple of minutes on a hot day. Here's what the handbook says about warm starting:

'Press the accelerator down slowly to supply the cylinders with a normal fuel mixture. Take care not to press the accelerator repeatedly, to avoid starting up the acceleration pumps, which would enrich the fuel mixture and could cause damping of the spark plug.'

But what about that frustrating moment when your Countach decides not to respond to your expert touch? (This usually occurs in front of an uninvited but interested audience.)
   Here is what the book advises (the bold-set words are theirs, the implication being that this will be an extraordinary and rare event):

'If the engine **fails to start**, the following may be the cause:
   The battery needs recharging.
   The starting mechanism is faulty (spark plugs dirty or worn out, spark coil damaged).
   The electric circuits are damaged or badly insulated.
   The slow-running jets are clogged.
   The fuel pumps are not working.'

Notice that the writer of this handbook is too polite to suggest that you, dear owner, have slipped up and failed to follow the procedure properly.

---

opening system. Nearly twenty years earlier, Mercedes-Benz had created the 'gullwing' door. Now Gandini and Lamborghini chose another upward-opening system, but with the hinge in roughly the normal position for a car door. These doors swing forwards and upwards, rather, as Stefano Pasini has observed, 'like a paper-cutter'. This was the first appearance of such a system in a production car, but it had earlier appeared on one of Bertone's most famous show cars, the Carabo of 1968 (based on Alfa Romeo mechanical components).

The show Countach had a makeshift

Giotto Bizzarrini

Born in 1927, Bizzarrini's car company of the early 1960s has been described by one knowledgeable commentator of the Italian sports car scene as 'a dilettante car producer, the Cizeta of its day'. He was, however, a brilliant engineer, having been in charge of the 250GTO at Ferrari (perhaps *the* classic sports racing Ferrari, and certainly the most expensive these days: one recently changed hands for £10 million), and he had also previously worked at Alfa Romeo.

The sensuous body shape of the GTO – influential in the shape of many subsequent sports coupes – was refined in the wind tunnel at Pisa, where Bizzarrini had studied engineering. This does not sound unusual today, but wind-tunnel shaping of cars was by no means universal in the late 1950s.

Remarkably, perhaps the finest and most lasting achievement of Bizzarrini's career was an engine which Ferrari had rejected. It was a four-camshaft V12 which he had designed for the 1.5-litre Formula 1. Ferruccio Lamborghini commissioned him to scale it up and design it for road use, and that is how the 350GTV engine – forerunner of all later Lamborghini V12s (except for the current Grand Prix engine), including that used in the Countach – was born. There is no substance to the suggestion made by one journalist that the original V12 was designed by Honda.

When Bizzarrini discovered that Lamborghini was not interested in motor racing, he left, having completed his side of the bargain profitably: his brief was to deliver an engine producing 350bhp. Any less than that and his fee would be cut; any more and he would receive a bonus. The engine which Dallara was given to refine for road use produced 358bhp at 9,800rpm on the dynamometer without problems. He calculated that more than 400bhp at 11,000rpm would have been achievable with larger carburettors.

In more recent years, Bizzarrini returned to Alfa Romeo, and was involved in the ugly but highly praised SZ. He is now once more an independent engineer, and his name has been linked with the sports car project which ex-Fiat boss Vittorio Ghidella has been working on for Ford.

interior, with an impractical steering-wheel, something to which the house of Bertone has returned on several occasions (the most bizarre example being the Athon), dissatisfied with the banal concept that a wheel should be circular and easily gripped by human hands. The instruments were fully electronic, displaying an attitude which still afflicts some manufacturers: we have the technology, so how are we going to use it? This is the reverse of proper engineering principles, in which a problem is identified, analysed and then the appropriate solution sought.

More practical minds were at work in the Countach's development team, and the production car from the start was fitted with a simple, round steering-wheel, and simple, round instruments. But the interior was only a degree or two more luxurious than that of the show prototype.

Some dislike the appearance of the Countach. It's a free country, up to a point anyway – but you certainly cannot ignore it. No car designer, before or since, has made such a dramatic visual statement. Even today a Countach – any model of Countach – produces a startled reaction from onlookers when it rolls up, unannounced and unexpected in the supermarket car park.

3 The Lamborghini Countach, 1971–1990

The Countach had been the undoubted star of the 1971 Geneva Show. But producing the 'car of the show' – and the car was no less sensational when displayed again the following year – is no guarantee of success in the market-place.

Having stimulated demand, it was now necessary for Lamborghini to turn this extraordinary 'dream car' into a product which could be exchanged, in showrooms with deep-pile carpets, for cheques sporting several zeros; and for the people who had written out the cheques to be able to drive happily away.

The task of development was down to Paolo Stanzani, the Chief Engineer at the factory, and to Bob Wallace, the Chief Test Driver. Especially in view of the fact that they carried out much of their work in a managerial vacuum, their achievements are all the more astounding.

It was to take almost three years to achieve the 'productionisation' of the Countach. If that seems a long time, remember that the original show car had really been slung together hastily, that the Countach was a complex design, and that it had to be made into a fast, safe and – within its own day-dream terms – practical car. It also had to comply with various legislative requirements, and even if those were fewer and less demanding than those of the 1990s, they nevertheless placed an additional burden upon the development team.

Finally, it had to be designed so that the factory could make money out of it. That is not as simple as it sounds, since although such cars are sold for very large sums, the complexity of construction, the large margins taken out by dealers – as well as being on the wrong end of the economies of scale equation – often make the search for profit a tough one – even if you do not choose to launch a gas-guzzling supercar in the middle of an oil crisis.

If you only make a few hundred – or perhaps even just a few dozen – cars per year, you cannot expect to obtain a beneficial rate for component prices from suppliers. Even in a craft factory like Lamborghini, where many components are manufactured within the premises, a substantial proportion must be bought in (quite apart from the raw materials of aluminium sheet, steel tubes, leather and so on), for example glass, lighting units, brake and clutch components, wiring looms, electrical/electronic components, instruments, and hundreds of seals and grommets and washers. But, realistically, not thousands, or millions of them . . .

PRACTICAL SOLUTIONS

Once the more fundamental engineering decisions on the car had been taken, a great

Bob Wallace

Born in Auckland, New Zealand, in 1938, Wallace brought to Lamborghini a down-to-earth, pragmatic approach which was precisely what the company needed at the time.

In late 1963, having spent several years as a racing mechanic for Maserati, Ferrari and smaller teams, he was considering an offer to return to Ferrari when he heard of the new Lamborghini car. He had earned a reputation as a useful test driver, and it was in this capacity that he started work for Lamborghini.

Soon, without having really planned it, he found himself in charge of the testing department, with four men working for him. A great deal of the testing was then conducted on public roads, and in those days there was no overall speed limit, but he also used the Dallara family's private race track and circuits like Misano and Varano.

Bob Wallace worked well with Lamborghini's two great engineers, Giampaolo Dallara and Paolo Stanzani. More than anyone else, he was responsible for sorting the handling and engineering of all Lamborghini cars from the beginning until he resigned in disgust in 1975.

Like most people at the time of his departure, including Stanzani, he did not believe that Lamborghini had a future. Today he lives in Phoenix, Arizona, where he makes his living from a garage business working on highly-tuned Italian cars, such as Lamborghinis.

– but it doesn't mean that the work was easy . . .

Engine cooling, as always in a mid-engined car, required a lot of attention, since there are difficulties associated with air-flow for rear-mounted radiators, especially when the car is stuck in low-speed traffic. Some of the purity of Gandini's design had to be abandoned at an early stage, and this was the birth of two enduring Countach features: the NACA ducts which begin at the trailing edge of the doors and lead into the rear wings; and the big 'air boxes' situated behind the side windows.

Bertone's idea of a periscopic rear-view mirror was abandoned early on in favour of a more conventional design; several types of windscreen wiper were tested (including a pair which 'clapped hands' in the centre of the screen) before the adoption of the single pantograph design; all the body panels had to be subtly altered for one reason or another; the use of NACA ducts led to a different type of door handle; and so on – thousands of little changes were brought about by the findings of the test team, or by product sourcing, or by the need to meet one regulation or another.

A small company above all needs a stable and consistent management to see it through such painstaking work, or else there is a danger of the project running away out of control. Lamborghini, as we have seen, did not have that kind of permanence at the time, so it is surprising – and a tribute to the work of those involved – that the early Countaches turned out as well as they did. Had men of the calibre of Stanzani and Wallace not been around, there would not be a Lamborghini car company today.

THE LP400 IS LAUNCHED

The first real Countach, now even officially called the LP400, appeared as a near-

deal of time-consuming work needed to be completed before production could be possible. Much of this development may seem minor, but that's often an inaccurate judgement based on a cursory examination of the solution to a particular problem: the more elegant the solution, the better the engineer

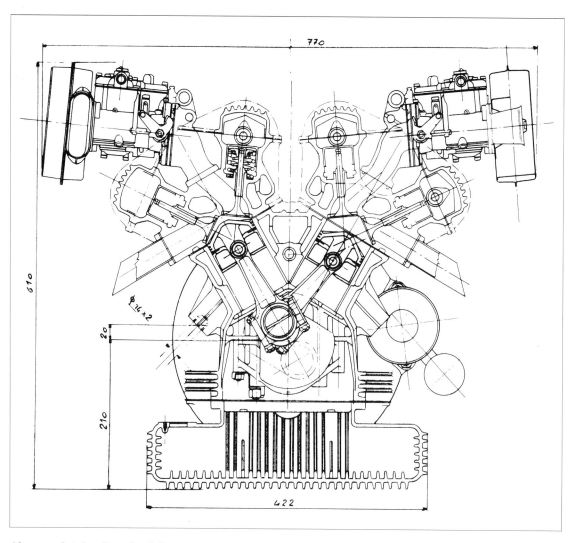

Above and right: *Spot the difference: two engineering drawings of the Countach engine from September 1971, showing that at that stage, a final choice had yet to be made of either crowned or flat-topped pistons.*

production car at the 1973 Geneva Show, and although it was much closer to the eventual production model than the hastily-finished prototype of two years earlier, it still required substantial work to be completed. It was not really until the third show car appeared, at Geneva in 1974, that the factory was able to produce a vehicle close in

almost all details to the eventual production model.

This 1974 show car at last had an entirely tubular frame, manufactured by specialist panel-builder Marchesi, and there were alterations to the shape of the side windows and the gauge of the aluminium bodywork among others. On 21 March 1974, the

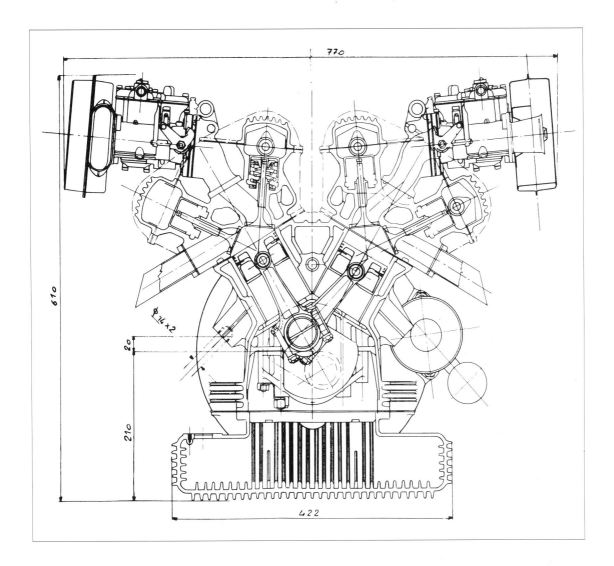

Countach passed crash tests at the Motor Industry Research Association (MIRA), near Nuneaton in Warwickshire, and on 21 April, the first Countach was delivered to a customer in Milan. The early production rate was very slow – only twenty-three cars were produced in 1974 – but by the standards of a few years later, that wasn't bad! Industrial unrest and uncertain management both played a significant part in this.

Despite the relatively small engine, with a capacity of 3,929cc, the power output was listed as 375bhp at 8,000rpm, which was enough to make the early Countach the quickest version of the car until the arrival of the 5000 *quattrovalvole*. It was apparently capable of almost 186mph (300kph), thanks largely to its very clean aerodynamic profile.

Lamborghini's V12 may require regular attention to keep it in the highest state of tune, but there has never been any question of its reliability and strength. These qualities were to play an important role in the

The Countach as it was when turned into a production car. This is an LP400. Notice that while the front end remains virtually unchanged, the periscope mirror has been abandoned, the slats behind the side window have been replaced by a small window and larger air intakes, and there is a NACA duct in the door/rear wing, concealing the revised door release.

A Bertone trademark (abandoned in later Countaches) was the sculpted line of the rear wheelarches, as seen in this LP400.

This is the LP400 back at the factory after front and rear crash tests in 1974. Despite the extensive mangling at each end, the cabin has stood up well to the impacts. Apparently the doors still opened and shut normally.

The Countach was designed for a tyre like the Pirelli P7, but no such rubber was available at its launch. Also to become a recognisable Countach feature was the five-slot alloy wheel, though the original rims were quite different.

survival of Lamborghini through its various financial/managerial crises. Customers were able to put up with a lack of the comfort provided by rival manufacturers because they were given a car that was basically rugged. But although the Countach was received well by both the press and by customers, there were still some who wanted more power and an even more aggressive appearance. Dallara produced two cars in 1976 which pointed the way ahead to future production versions.

Beginning with the tyres, the standard car's Michelins (205/70 on the front 7.5J rims, and 215/70 on the rear 9J wheels, with a diameter of 14in (356mm)) were replaced by the new Pirelli P7s. Bob Wallace has said that this at last made the Countach in most respects what it should have been from the start. The Countach had been in effect designed for P7s before these became available. There was no choice for the first Countach but to opt for the Michelin XWX,

bearing a higher profile and the 14in (356mm) rims, which necessitated smaller brakes. If it is an exaggeration to suggest that this ruined the first Countach, it is undeniable that it severely compromised its potential.

It was in this era that tyre manufacturers were beginning to transfer the knowledge gained from racing into a new generation of low-profile, high performance road tyres. These P7s were fitted to 15in (381mm) diameter wheels (8.5J at the front and 12J at the rear), and their aspect ratios were 225/50 at the front and 345/35 at the rear. These required widened arches to accommodate them, and Dallara made this a special feature, adding moulded glass fibre extensions to cover them. At the front, he fitted a new air dam, and for the first time, that Formula 1-inspired fashion gimmick, the large rear wing, mounted on two vertical fins, was added. This has never been necessary for improved stability; it destroys much of the limited ability of the rear-view mirror, and it actually robs the car of much of its performance in the upper part of the speed range; but some customers (even Keke Rosberg, one of several Grand Prix drivers to have owned a Countach) believe it adds to the car's beauty. Many other customers, such as Grand Prix driver Pierluigi Martini, disagree.

The two cars were built to special order: one for an Italian, who chose red for the exterior and a black interior; the other ordered by Grand Prix team owner Walter Wolf, a flamboyant Austro-Canadian millionaire. This turned out to be a superb piece of publicity for Lamborghini, as the car

Right: A production Countach LP400 from 1975. Gandini's original design is still clearly visible, despite the enlarged air scoops above the rear wings to improve cooling and the addition of curved panes behind the door windows for better all-round vision.

Motor testing the right-hand drive LP400 at MIRA's proving ground at Nuneaton in 1975. This is on the 'Number 2' circuit, and the combination of tyre marks and the position of the car (facing the wrong way) leads ineluctably to the conclusion that a spin has just occurred.

appeared in the paddock of the world's Grand Prix races.

WOLF INSPIRES THE LP400S

Wolf's car was painted light Bugatti blue, with gold-painted wheels and gold pinstriping, and had a natural leather interior. This car, chassis no 202, is probably the most famous Lamborghini in the world, and was even used by Tamiya for marketing a 1:12 scale model of the Countach S. In fact, Wolf's car gave the factory more publicity than it could cope with, and it was difficult to keep up with the volume of orders for the LP400. So a 'productionised' version of these special Dallara models was not immediately put into action.

In the late 1970s, as we have seen, the factory was struggling, with largely absentee management. Against this background, the Countach LP400S was introduced without much ceremony at the 1978 Geneva Show. Essentially, this was an up-dated LP400 to which some of the modifications made on the two special cars had been applied: the bigger tyres on a new design of wheel, with widened, more angular arches; an altered roof-line, with the characteristic groove removed to increase headroom; new instruments from Jaeger; and a more honest appraisal of engine power (dropped from 375 to 353bhp). The increased aerodynamic drag of the frontal design lowered top speed by at least 15.5mph (25kph), and the increase in weight had a damaging effect on acceleration; but roadholding improved.

Walter Wolf was wooed by the factory as a possible saviour of Lamborghini, but he declined the opportunity to pour his fortune into such an interesting bottomless pit, having already blown a lot of it away in the costly exercise of not winning Grand Prix races. Possibly, he would only have accepted ownership of Lamborghini if he had been allowed to change its name to Wolf.

ENTER THE LP500S

The Mimran management era began early in 1980: French businessmen Patrick and Jean-Claude Mimran had rescued Lamborghini from a string of management failures and bankruptcy. (*See* Chapter 8).

Although sales of the LP400S were holding up well (there was now a consistent supply of parts to build them), and production was gradually increasing to satisfy demand, it was becoming apparent that Lamborghini was slipping behind some of its competitors, notably Ferrari, whose Boxer's engine was now of 5-litre capacity. The Countach's 4-litre engine simply lacked the grunt to push its aggressive bodyshell through the air with the efficiency to claim the title of the world's fastest car. Some individual customers had their engines upgraded, but the new management team was unsatisfied.

An intensive development programme began, the first result of which appeared from chassis no 1121312 onwards: the roof was raised by 1.2in (30mm) to accommodate taller drivers and as a taller than average driver, I can tell you that this makes a substantial difference. The engine capacity was increased to 4,754cc to obtain a significant increase in power. This was the LP500S, also known as the 5000, which was 12mph (20kph) faster than its predecessor,

and had improved handling. The top speed of 180mph (290kph) was enough to see off any rival, and the only car that could out-accelerate it was the Porsche 911 Turbo.

...FOLLOWED BY THE 5000 *QUATTRO-VALVOLE*

In 1982 Alfieri began work on the 7-litre version of the Countach engine, for use in the LM and powerboats. (The LM is a large off-road vehicle which makes a Land Rover look like a toy. Originally designed for military use, it has become a popular leisure vehicle in the USA.) The engine was successful, but unsuitable for use in the Countach itself: it was too large and heavy. Alfieri has claimed responsibility for the *quattrovalvole*, but those in the know suggest that it was not in fact his work. Apparently, although a great engineer in his time, he had by now become old-fashioned in his ideas, and he was later to set back development of the Diablo by at least a year. However, that is rushing forward.

It was decided that an increase in power was necessary, to anticipate developments from rival manufacturers. Turbocharging was considered as a means of extracting extra power, but was rejected because the limited space within the car's engine compartment made it an impractical solution — even without the two intercoolers which would be required. Instead, Lamborghini chose a 48-valve development of the engine; at this time, 4-valves-per-cylinder heads, though nothing new, were gaining favour throughout the industry.

Development continued throughout 1984. Although no radical changes were made to the construction of the bottom end from the previous 24-valve version, important dimensional alterations were made to maximise the capability of the new engine: the bore was unchanged, at 85.5mm, but the stroke

*By the late 1980s, the factory attempted to dissuade customers
from fitting the rear wing, but some simply wouldn't listen.*

The LP400 looks dated today only because of its relatively narrow tyres.

Above, left and opposite:
Lamborghini's LM002 four-wheel-drive vehicle, with Countach-based engine, did not find favour with the world's armies despite its ability to cross rough ground at 125mph (201kph). By 1989, though, it was in popular demand as another toy for the mega-rich, and was useful to the factory in taking up the slack caused by the cessation of Jalpa production.

A device for lighting cigars with £50 notes in a hurricane: the Lamborghini offshore powerboat, about to be transported, with a spare Countach-derived engine or two, to Cowes in 1986.

was increased from 69 to 75mm, giving a swept volume of 5,167cc (from 4,754cc). So, for the first time, the swept volume exceeded that projected for the original show car, with its fanciful 'LP500' title. The compression ratio was raised from 9.2 to 9.5:1.

The power output rose from 375 to a minimum of 455bhp at 7,000rpm, and the torque to a peak of 369lb ft at 5,200rpm. Again, this was the first time that the figures hoped for back in 1971 had been beaten. Some engines produced 470bhp on the test bench. Also, the flat spots in the power curves of the 3,929 and 4,754cc engines had been eradicated.

Bodywork changes for the *quattrovalvole* included front and rear lids constructed from Kevlar, with a large, central 'power bulge' built into the engine cover. Pirelli's new P7R tyres were used – still 345/35 VR 15 at the rear, but increased at the front from 205/50 VR 15 to 225/50 VR 15. One of the objectives here was to reduce initial understeer. This was not only lighter than the conventional steel frame and aluminium panels, but it also (because of the reduced bulk) permitted greater interior space.

The 5000QV, possibly *the* definitive Countach, instantly became the fastest production car in the world, if one ignores limited-edition models such as Ferrari's GTO (and later the F40) and the Porsche 959. The important comparison is with the Testarossa, and the Countach is not only substantially more powerful, but also quite different in character. The Testarossa is a beautiful car, very comfortable, fast, and superbly built. But it isn't aimed at the type of customer by whom the Countach will be most appreciated. Compared with the Countach, the Testarossa's suspension is softer,

and its cornering power is hampered by a high centre of gravity. The Lamborghini makes fewer concessions to comfort (not that it is actually uncomfortable) and it is certainly less practical than the Ferrari. All in all, the Ferrari is a less 'aggressive' car than the Countach.

By now, the LM's 7-litre engine had grown to 8 litres in the process of development for marine use, and its power output was 700bhp. Renato Dalla Valle dominated the 1985 European Offshore Powerboat Championship using this engine, and it has gone on to further successes since then.

THE *EVOLUZIONE*

Towards the end of 1987, an unusual-looking car began to appear in the 'scoop' pages of the world's motoring magazines. That it was based on the Countach would have been obvious even if the photographs had not been taken near the factory. Yet – just as obviously – there were differences. The car had strange wheel-trims and it appeared that the unpainted body was made partly of composites, as was indeed the case. These modifications exaggerated the standard Countach's air of crouching malevolence.

Some of the stories suggested that this was the prototype of the next Countach, a far from unreasonable assumption. But that was entirely incorrect. The full story emerged soon enough, and it was a fascinating one.

The car, known as the *Evoluzione* (Evolution), was not itself ever intended as a production prototype of any kind nor as a potential production car, but it was more than a blind alley. It was, however, designed, built and extensively used as a test-bed for various engineering and production ideas. Perhaps the most interesting of these was the construction of the body/chassis unit. The Countach's complex tubular

chassis was not used, and instead, Lamborghini's engineers built a chassis/body out of composites. This consisted of the cockpit, including the floor and roof, the central 'tunnel', sills and front and rear bulkheads. This structure was built in one piece, from a honeycomb and aluminium foil sandwich material, Kevlar and carbon fibre bonded together under partial vacuum at a temperature of 284°F (140°C).

The front lid and rear cover, and the front air dam/bumper and the wheelarches, were also made of composites. Aluminium panels were used for the wings and doors. Overall, the car was almost 860lb (390kg) lighter than standard, though that was partly due to its being untrimmed and short of various pieces of equipment which a normal Countach owner – if that is not a contradiction in terms – would regard as essential. Apart from air-conditioning (by then for a long time a standard item in the Countach), carpets and sound-proofing materials, these deleted 'extras' included a windscreen wiper and washer, headlights, a horn, and a speedometer. Needless to say, these trivial details did not deter Lamborghini's test staff from using the car on public roads.

The composite material worked very well as a noise-absorbing structure, so that despite the absence of trim and other materials, the *Evoluzione* was apparently not much louder to be in than a standard Countach (though one writer disagreed). According to Paul Frère (who wrote about his drive in the car in *Motor*, 9 January 1988) it gave the impression of being entirely rigid.

The sills had air intakes built into them which after alterations soon found their way into production in the Countach Anniversary. The Anniversary also had more composite panels than the 5000QV. The flat wheel-trims were excellent for aerodynamic purposes, but would not have been suitable for production, because of their inefficiency in permitting the brakes to cool.

With a 'blue-printed' engine delivering

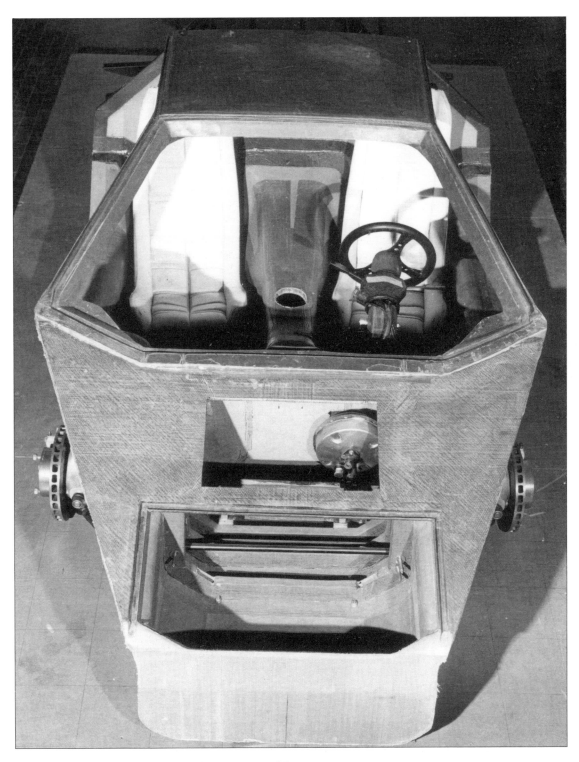

The Evoluzione *was thought to be the prototype of the next* Countach. *A large proportion of the chassis/body was made of composites.*

The Evoluzione *sported aluminium panels for wings and doors as well as futuristic wheel-trims.*

some 500bhp, and with standard transmission (except that the gate had been altered, giving a shorter 'throw' between gears), the *Evoluzione* is claimed to have achieved the 'magic' 200mph (322kph) at the Nardo test track in southern Italy; so it would be even faster in a straight line.

In the end, the *Evoluzione* is no more. It was barrier-tested (that is destroyed) 'for internal information'. Apart from the cost and complexity of building a car by these methods (similar to those used in Grand Prix chassis), production was ruled out for two reasons. First, although exceptionally good at protecting the occupants in the event of a major accident (as proven by Gerhard Berger's horrific-looking accident in his Ferrari at Imola in 1989, which would not have

been survivable in a Grand Prix car of only a few years ago), it is then no more than junk. It cannot be repaired, and a new shell is required. Even Lamborghini owners would find difficulty in paying the insurance premiums. A second problem is that composite materials age and decay in a less predictable, less curable, and above all less observable manner than steel or steel and aluminium.

At one time, the *Evoluzione* was also used for testing electronically-controlled damping and ride height, ABS brakes, four-wheel drive with a variable torque split, and even a fully-retractable wiper system. So although nothing quite like the *Evoluzione* will ever be built as a production car at Sant'Agata, it served its purpose first as a confirmation of how they did *not* want to

Right and below: *Distinctively styled (by Pininfarina), the Ferrari Testarossa is no match for the Countach as a supercar. Though well engineered, it is softer and milder, aimed at a less demanding, less sporty customer.*

Engine/Transmission Development

Lamborghini's four-cam V12 engine had already been in production for eight years when the Countach was first shown in prototype form in 1971. In varying capacities and states of tune it had powered every Lamborghini – the 350GT, 400GT, Islero, Jarama, Espada and Miura.

Bizzarrini's original design for Lamborghini was very 'peaky' and although it apparently produced nearly 360bhp at 9,800rpm on the dyno, it was too much of a racer to go straight into a production car. Accordingly, as used in the 350GTV show car, it was detuned and 'civilised' by Dallara to produce 260bhp from its 3,465cc. From the 400GT onwards, the swept volume increased to 3,929cc, and the power output steadily rose, to a peak of 385bhp (at 7,850rpm) in the Miura P400SV. Incidentally, the journalist Leonard Setright has suggested that the original Bizzarrini/ Dallara V12 was designed for Lamborghini by Honda. No substantiation was offered in support of this theory, and all the evidence seems to contradict it. Everyone at Lamborghini finds the story amusing, and American writer Pete Lyons in his *The Complete Book of Lamborghini* attributes the theory to 'a lazy afternoon with a bottle of Lambrusco'.

It was, eventually, an engine of similar dimensions which was used in the first Countaches: with its bore of 82mm and 62mm stroke, the LP400 engine has one of the highest bore/stroke ratios (1.32:1) of any production engine in history, and was outstanding in this respect in its day.

Today, only one engine is significantly higher up the scale, and that is Maserati's 2.8-litre V6, at 1.40:1. The Oldsmobile Quad-4 2.5-litre four-cylinder and the 5,995cc Cizeta V16-T (not a production engine, to be sure), are just ahead of the LP400, on 1.33:1. Two which equal it are the 2.7-litre version of Porsche's 944 engine and the 4.3-litre Rover-based V-8 used in some TVRs.

Stanzani's principal motive in wishing to enlarge this elegant 3.9-litre engine for the Countach was to maintain a respectable power output while meeting existing and future emissions regulations – at that time, American regulations were beginning to take hold. The bore of his new engine was 85mm and the stroke 73mm. This would have given the 'LP500' a more powerful, but a lazier engine. On the test-bed, the 4,971cc 'LP500' motor apparently produced 440bhp (DIN) at 7,400rpm and 366lb of torque at 5,000rpm.

Although the new car's engine shared Lamborghini's traditional internal dimensions, it was very much altered. A new sump had had to be designed, incorporating a sealed driveshaft from the gearbox to the differential. Apart from any other reasons, it is to be welcomed that this sump found its way into production simply because of the constructional beauty of the external ribbing. The new engine block was also used in the production car, suitably modified.

Although the main reason for turning the engine through 90 degrees was to improve high-speed stability, with a better gearchange as the second major motive, it gave the incidental benefits of a simplified and more efficient exhaust system, and better access for servicing, especially to the distributors, alternator, timing chains and water pump, but also to the spark plugs and carburettors. Making minor adjustments in the area of the forward bank of cylinders of a Miura engine *in situ* must be a mechanic's nightmare.

Everything that has since happened to the Countach engine has been part of a process of gradual refinement in order to meet new regulations, to increase horsepower without using more fuel, and to seek improvements, however small, because that's what genuine engineers always strive for. With the arrival of the 5000QV, the Countach at last had an engine which – with the aid of improved breathing (thanks to its four big valves per cylinder and an improved exhaust system) and electronic management of the ignition – actually exceeded Stanzani's specification for the 'LP500'.

Undoubtedly more functional, it isn't quite as externally pretty as in the past: although the ribbing remains on the gearbox casing, it has gone from the sump, which is now a plain casting. What a shame – but it must be significantly cheaper to manufacture. It is interesting to note that the 5000QV shares one obvious ancillary design feature with the 'LP500': it has one twelve-plug distributor, driven off the lower left-side camshaft; the production LP400 had two six-plug distributors, each driven by one of the left-side camshafts.

As for the future, it has been predicted that the existing engine's output of 88PS per litre specific power (already high by road-car standards) could be improved to 100, with the peak power output rising to 515bhp.

build cars, and second as a test-hack for components which will form part of future production.

COUNTACH PRODUCTION

Exactly how many Countaches have been produced since the first, so-called 'LP500' was displayed at Geneva in 1971 we shall probably never know. The Lamborghini factory in those days was – unconsciously –

more concerned with creating a heritage, and with staying in business from one week to the next, than with keeping accurate records for posterity.

It is only in recent years that more interest has been shown in the historical aspects, and I am very grateful to Dott Stefano Pasini (eye specialist, Lamborghini enthusiast and Editor of *Rivista Lamborghini*, a magazine produced with the official approval of the Lamborghini company) for the following figures:

1981 LP5000S

From every angle, the Countach is an interesting piece of sculpture in which form is narrowly beaten into second place by function.

Model	Year(s)	Number produced
'LP500'	(1971 Geneva Show car)	1
LP400	1973–1978	156
LP400S	1979–1982	237
LP500S	1982–1984	190
5000QV	1985–1988	450 (approximate)
Anniversary	1988–1989	450 (estimate)

Jean-Francois Marchet and the late Pete Coltrin, in their book on the Countach, suggested the following annual production figures, which do not add up, as far as I can see. They evidently made sense to somebody, because they were left unchanged when the book was re-printed.

LP400

1974	23
1975	60
1976	27
1977	40

This, as Marchet and Coltrin pointed out, produces a total of 150, which is six (or perhaps seven) fewer than the figure I have been given. At least up to this point, even if there is a minor disagreement, the figures are intelligible. But from here on, the figures given by Marchet and Coltrin seem to zoom beyond my mathematical comprehension.

LP400S

1978	16
1979	40
1980	120

Yet Marchet and Coltrin suggested that this added up to 385. . .

LP500S

1981	88
1982	96
1983	114
1984	132

Marchet and Coltrin declared that this added up to 325.

4 The Anniversary

To celebrate the extraordinary quarter century since Ferruccio Lamborghini had become a car manufacturer, the factory introduced in 1988 the first production model since the Chrysler takeover: the Countach Anniversary.

As an aside, Lamborghini also held a most extraordinary, and very Italian, party to celebrate this momentous event. Numbers had to be restricted because of over-subscription, but Lamborghini owners came from all over the world, with their cars. It was a tremendous party, lasting several days and spread over three locations (the factory, a small spa town, and the Monza race circuit on the final day of the Italian Grand Prix practice).

I had the honour to be invited to judge a 'beauty contest' of Lamborghinis. Of course it was quite impossible, with more than 100 mostly shiny cars (with the occasional 'in good running order' example going past) to form any kind of fair judgement. How do you decide which Lamborghini model is the most beautiful? Having done so, more or less, how do you choose between half a dozen which, without a thorough workshop inspection, all look equally immaculate? It is of course, impossible, and the 'judges' had to resort to expert guidance from a guiding light of the Lamborghini Owners' Club to avoid causing offence. (Probably no one would have minded anyway, as it was an event designed for amusement rather than serious competition.) There were two highlights of the party. One was a dinner in Salsomaggiore which was attended by several hundred Lamborghini owners, dealers and others; and the guest of honour was Ferruccio himself. A splendid opportunity was lost – the wine was Italian, but it did not bear the Lamborghini label.

The other 'peak' of this event was the opportunity for around 100 Lamborghinis, including more than a dozen Countaches, to turn a couple of parade laps around the Monza circuit. At one point, cruising along an *autostrada* in a Silhouette, I was overtaken by seven Countaches in a line, all in high gear with lots of revs. It is a moment I'll never forget, if I live to be 100.

It was at the anniversary party at the factory that the Anniversary model was officially unveiled. Some people like its appearance, but the majority view seems to be mildly unfavourable. I dislike it quite a lot in comparison with either the first Countach or the wingless version of the QV; those to me are the greatest versions of the car. On the other hand, I wouldn't mind being one of the 400 or so fortunate customers. I'd live in a make-believe world until the first service was due, and then sell at a vast profit. (The trouble with a car like the Countach is that, just to pay the insurance premiums and running costs, you need to be in the first division of earners, rather than in the relegation zone of the second division.)

Essentially, the Anniversary has the same panels as the 5000QV – with which it shares its mechanical components – but they are partially disguised by composite additions (the word 'excrescences' seems too unkind). These include the carbon fibre front bumper and the air dam – the latter a rabbit warren

Overleaf: *Around 100 Lamborghinis did a couple of parade laps of the Monza circuit the day before the 1988 Italian Grand Prix, as part of Lamborghini's 25th anniversary celebrations.*

*Front cover of Lamborghini's limited edition brochure to
celebrate the company's 25th anniversary.*

of holes, including some new ones on the sides to cool the front brakes – new sills – based on those tested on the *Evoluzione* – which have straked ducts to take air to the rear brakes, and a new type of 'air box' on the top of each rear wing. This looks as if it might be based, for sentimental reasons, on one of the extractor outlets of a tractor factory. After all, Ferruccio also had a heating and air-conditioning business.

At the rear, the magnificent trapezoidal feel of the tail-light cluster is spoiled by the special American add-on energy-absorbent material and also by the rear bumper, again made of carbon fibre.

I rather like the new composite road wheels, which cleverly continue the five-circle theme which began with the introduction of the LP500S. But overall, one can safely say that it is time to go back to the drawing board: it was asking too much to meet 1990s safety regulations while preserving an early 1970s shape.

Phillip Bingham got a ride in the car in Italy for *Fast Lane* (his article appeared in the January 1989 issue), or rather two rides – first with test driver Biagio Vigorati (and could there be a better name for a brave Italian test pilot?) and then with Sandro Munari, the former world-class rally driver

A lot of information crammed into a confined space: interior of a right-hand-drive Countach Anniversary. Not many owners will get the speedometer needle close to the end of the 199mph (320kph) scale.

Lamborghinis from all over the world gathered outside the factory for the anniversary party.

Right: *Lee Iacocca of Chrysler with the car which was named to mark Lamborghini's first quarter-century, and which was also designed as the last Countach.*

Below: *Barry Robinson, a long-time Lamborghini fan, has owned several Countaches. This, complete with personalised number-plate, is his Anniversary model.*

The Anniversary's tail-light covers were, alas, taken from the US-specification quattrovalvole.

who now works for Lamborghini as a combined test driver and PR man. Munari should be quite used to sitting in the claustrophobic cockpits of cars designed by Gandini/Bertone, since many of his successes were at the wheel of a Lancia Stratos.

Bingham put the new body shape into the context of the motor industry and the way it operates:

'Enthusiasts and romantics alike will regard the new Countach Anniversary as a tribute to the determination of Ferrucio Lamborghini . . . Purists might also view the Anniversary as the apotheosis of the 17-year-old Countach theme, the greatest ever derivative of a durably great supercar. Doubtless, some affluent forward thinkers will smother the car in wraps and squirrel it away. Which, of course, would be missing the point entirely. Industry observers may see the Anniversary in a slightly different light; a calculated cosmetic exercise, a tactic intended to prevent demand (and an 18-month waiting list) from flagging when attentions might otherwise be directed towards the Countach's 1990 replacement, the Diablo. And some will say, perhaps rightly, that the Anniversary is the first evidence of marketing input from America, an indication that Chrysler calls the tune.'

I think, with the benefit of hindsight, that the comments about the Chrysler marketing input were not correct, but bearing in mind the feud which was then being conducted between Detroit and Sant'Agata, it would surprise me if any of the Italian members of the Lamborghini management would be disappointed to read such a suggestion.

Bingham also reported on the more comfortable seats:

The Anniversary's attractive three-piece wheels carry on the five-slot tradition, while the P Zero tyres improve both grip and handling behaviour. However, 15in diameter rims are small by today's standards (16in is the norm for a high-performance car, and 17in is increasingly popular). One effect is to limit the size of the brake discs, which are satisfactory for road use but soon fade on a racing circuit.

Television star: the Countach
Anniversary appeared in a stylish
commercial for Pirelli.

Right: *The Anniversary looks as good
in the studio as it does on the road.*

'Gone are the Countach's austere, one-piece bucket seats which forced your buttocks down low, your knees up high, and a pronounced curvature to your spine whether you liked it or not. Instead, wider, comfortably padded chairs upholstered in expensive-looking leather have independent seat cushions and back rests. Electrically controlled by switches tucked under a flap in each door's armrest, they offer a perfectly reasonable range of height, fore/aft, and rake adjustment. These condescensions to luxury are at the expense of hip-hugging lateral support, although you can't slide too far in a Countach seat before bumping up against a door armrest one side or the transmission tunnel the other.'

I shall take Bingham's word for this. The only occasion on which I have sat inside a standard Anniversary was on a motor show stand where no one could find the keys to the ignition; so it was impossible to move the electrically-adjustable seat.

One of the most important changes to the Anniversary is the adoption of Pirelli P-Zero tyres. They are actually the same size as the previously-used standard P7s (225/50 ZR 15 at the front, and 345/35 ZR 15 at the rear), but apparently these, in conjunction with quite small suspension adjustments, make a significant improvement to on-limit handling. These were Sandro Munari's comments, comparing the Anniversary with the 5000QV: 'If you drive hard, the Anniversary is definitely quicker out of a corner. You don't have to wait so long before going on the power. And through the corner there is more grip and a much nicer balance. It is easier now. You know how the car will react in every condition . . . In Italy we have a word for it. *Sincera*. It doesn't hide anything from you any more. It is fair and it is honest.'

The Anniversary is the last Countach, the last car from the factory which is still, in its essentials, closely related to the one that Ferruccio Lamborghini signed off for production in May 1972 (though the V12, in modified form, lives on, let us hope, forever). It may also be the last car of its type to be produced anywhere in the world. We will not see its like again. Perhaps the Countach, as *Autocar* suggested in 1973, really is 'the last of the Supercars'.

DRIVING THE ANNIVERSARY AT BRANDS HATCH

Although motoring journalists drive numerous cars in the course of their work, opportunities to drive a Lamborghini Countach are rare. To most writers it is an irritating gap in their experience, though it doesn't stop some of them expressing opinions.

I once counted up the cars I had driven in one year, and was amazed to find that it was more than 100. It is fortunate that I make numerous notes, because otherwise many of the Toyotas and Nissans and other products of Japan PLC would blur into each other in the recesses of the mind. But even without notes, the rare cars, like an Aston Martin Vantage, Bentley Turbo R or Ferrari Testarossa imprint themselves indelibly on even the least retentive memory because of their distinctive characters.

As for a Countach, that is something else. If you cannot recall all the details of your drive in a Countach, then you've probably forgotten your own name.

By coincidence, at the point of writing this book, I had the chance to drive a Countach Anniversary at Brands Hatch. This was several firsts for me: the first Countach I had driven in Britain, the first Anniversary model, and my first drive in a Countach around a racing circuit.

We had the car at Brands for an audio tape we were recording for *Fast Lane*. The other cars on the tape are an Aston Martin Vantage, Porsche 959 and 7-litre Lister Jaguar.

The Anniversary has a new type of 'air box' on the top of each rear wing.

Even after having seen so many Countaches (and I had been at the factory in Sant'Agata only one week previously) I still find the sight of the car astonishing. It has an animal quality absent from most modern rivals. Though to me the 5000QV (minus wing) is the epitome of the Countach shape, and I'm not keen on the modified air intakes and add-on skirts and valences, the Anniversary is just as imposing. Yet it's amazing how small it looks when you place it alongside, for example, an Aston Martin Vantage.

I'm still not sure whether I agree with the recommended manner of entering a Countach (rear-end on seat, and then swing legs inside). It seems easier for me, with my long legs, to slide my left leg in below the steering-wheel and then drag remaining elements in

Overleaf: *A flash of red. It is interesting to compare this side view of the Anniversary with the Diablo (see Chapter 6). It is almost as if the Countach had deliberately been made ungainly in appearance in order to make its successor look even more attractive in comparison.*

after it. Especially for a tall driver it is necessary to take care not to bash your skull either on the up-lifted door or on the roof itself.

However, once inside, there is more space than might be imagined – especially in this version – with its sports seats. These are an option which can be added after purchase, so the electric adjustment buttons remain, even though they are redundant with these slimmer, lower seats. If you specify them, you can keep the original seats, and sell the car with both sets. It seems fairly ridiculous to have electrically-adjustable seats in a car like this anyway. But that is not the most absurd fitting: the Countach's 'letterbox' opening windows are now electrically powered. Yes, two little electric motors to create openings just large enough to put your hand through.

On the other hand, the air conditioning system is not another example of extravagant over-equipping. It is virtually an essential, to avoid roasting the car's occupants on a hot day, and it also performs the task of demisting the huge windscreen quite effectively.

The main advantage of the sports seats is a small increase in both leg-room and head-room. Leg space in the car is surprisingly good, and there is a gap above my head just large enough for comfortable road driving; however, helmets were compulsory on the circuit and this forced my neck into an awkward tilt.

The driving position is not perfect by any means, however. Always in a mid-engined car, the single significant advantage of left-hand drive over sitting on the British side of a car becomes obvious: wheelarch intrusion imposes an offset of the seat from the pedals. For left-hand drive this is not important because it is the right leg which can be held in a straight line alongside the central 'tunnel', while the left foot can be braced against a rest set into the inner arch.

When the car is converted for our use, the leg which operates throttle and brake is in an awkward position, while there is no convenient place to rest the left foot when it is not being used to operate the clutch pedal. This is not a matter of comfort alone, because to drive a car properly you need to be well braced inside it. This is especially important in a powerful car at a circuit like Brands Hatch, where substantial *g*-force is generated almost all the way round the so-called 'Indy' Circuit.

There can be two additional drawbacks, both related to the action of the pedals. In some cars, mostly front-engined ones with cramped engine bays, it is impossible to switch the brake servo to the ideal position in which the pedal acts directly upon it, and this can spoil both the feel and efficiency of the brakes; Volkswagens in particular have suffered from this over the years. In the Countach, as in most mid-engined cars, the servo is simply switched from one side of the car to the other.

However, it does suffer from the other problem, which is an alteration in the throttle linkage. British Countaches vary in this respect, but the effect in our test car at Brands was extreme, at least at very low speeds: the resistance of the throttle pedal was higher than that of the brakes in some small cars, and although that is not a serious problem once the car is moving rapidly, it does make application of power at low speeds, especially when pulling away from rest, rather difficult.

I was told by a representative of Portman Lamborghini, the British importers, that it was necessary to dismantle this car's linkage and reassemble it to bring it up to the required standard. But there is no doubt that left-hand drive cars possess a small, yet significant, advantage in this respect, which has a serious impact upon driveability. Driving a Countach at low speeds and in confined spaces is a pretty miserable experience. The steering lock is poor, the clutch and brakes are heavy, and visibility, especially for reversing, is dismal.

In the Countach, you can have an engine that breathes efficiently or you can have an internal rear-view mirror that performs a useful function: for the Anniversary, priority was given to the former.

However, get it on to a suitable stretch of road, and your opinions can change very rapidly. Apart from all the other qualities of the car, the engine is simply wonderful, with a unique blend of refinement and aggression. By comparison, a standard Jaguar V12 is nearly silent, while a highly tuned one, such as the 7-litre Lister engine, conveys a more overt sense of violence. It is not that the Countach engine is quiet, by any means, and having a stereo system inside one seems singularly pointless.

Highly impressive is the feeling of solidity. A spaceframe chassis may be 'old hat' these days, but the Countach cannot be far short of the rigidity achieved by the theoretically superior monocoques. I could hear no creaks or rattles in this well used car – which had covered some 8,000 miles (12,870km) – and there was virtually no wind roar. Not surprisingly, the big tyres were far from silent over changes of surface, and this was more noticeable in a brief drive on the roads near the circuit.

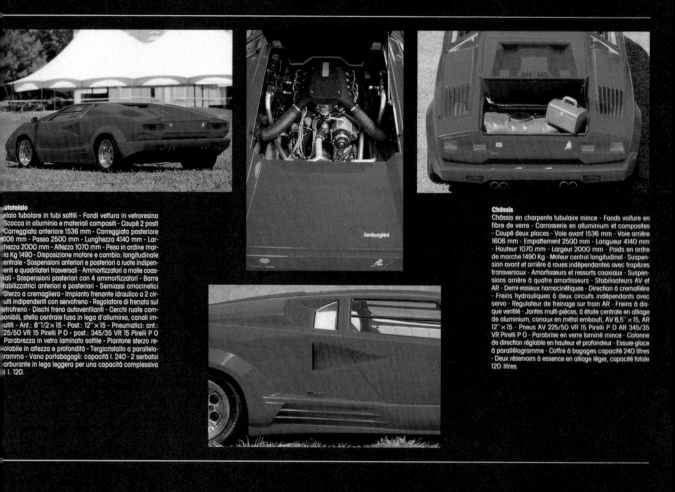

utotelaio
elaio tubolare in tubi sottili - Fondi vettura in vetroresina
Scocca in alluminio e materiali compositi - Coupé 2 posti
Carreggiata anteriore 1536 mm - Carreggiata posteriore
606 mm - Passo 2500 mm - Lunghezza 4140 mm - Lar-
hezza 2000 mm - Altezza 1070 mm - Peso in ordine mar-
ia Kg 1490 - Disposizione motore e cambio: longitudinale
entrale - Sospensioni anteriori e posteriori a ruote indipen-
enti e quadrilateri trasversali - Ammortizzatori a molle coas-
iali - Sospensioni posteriori con 4 ammortizzatori - Barre
tabilizzatrici anteriori e posteriori - Semiassi omocinetici
Sterzo a cremagliera - Impianto frenante idraulico a 2 cir-
uiti indipendenti con servofreno - Regolatore di frenata sul
etrofreno - Dischi freno autoventilanti - Cerchi ruote com-
onibili, stella centrale fusa in lega d'alluminio, canali im-
utili - Ant.: 8"1/2×15 - Post.: 12"×15 - Pneumatici: ant.:
25/50 VR 15 Pirelli P O - post.: 345/35 VR 15 Pirelli P O
Parabrezza in vetro laminato sottile - Piantone sterzo re-
olabile in altezza e profondità - Tergicristallo a parallelo-
ramma - Vano portabagagli: capacità l. 240 - 2 serbatoi
arburante in lega leggera per una capacità complessiva
i l. 120.

Châssis
Châssis en charpente tubulaire mince - Fonds voiture en
fibre de verre - Carrosserie en alluminium et composites
- Coupé deux places - Voie avant 1536 mm - Voie arrière
1606 mm - Empattement 2500 mm - Longueur 4140 mm
- Hauteur 1070 mm - Largeur 2000 mm - Poids en ordre
de marche 1490 Kg - Moteur central longitudinal - Suspension avant et arrière à roues indépendantes avec trapèzes
transversaux - Amortisseurs et ressorts coaxiaux - Suspen-
sions arrière à quatre amortisseurs - Stabilisateurs AV et
AR - Demi-essieux homocinétiques - Direction à crémaillère
- Freins hydrauliques à deux circuits indépendants avec
servo - Regulateur de freinage sur train AR - Freins à dis-
que ventilé - Jantes multi-pièces, à étoile centrale en alliage
de aluminium, canaux en métal embouti, AV 8,5" ×15, AR
12"×15 - Pneus AV 225/50 VR 15 Pirelli P O AR 345/35
VR Pirelli P O - Parabrise en verre laminé mince - Colonne
de direction réglable en hauteur et profondeur - Essuie glace
à parallélogramme - Coffre à bagages capacité 240 litres
- Deux réservoirs à essence en alliage léger, capacité totale
120 litres.

*These details of the Anniversary are taken from Lamborghini's
25th anniversary brochure.*

Chassis
Tubular frame - Fiberglass floor panels - Aluminium and composites body - 2 seater coupe - Track, front 1536 mm, rear 1606 mm - Wheelbase 2500 mm - Lenght 4140 mm - Width 2000 mm - Height 1070 mm - Weight in running order 1490 Kg - Mid-engine, longitudinal layout - Independent front and rear suspension with transverse A-arms, damper and coaxial springs - Rear suspension with two damper units per wheel - Front and rear stabiliser bars - Constant-moving driveshafts - Rack and pinion steering - Dual independent hydraulic brakes with booster - Brake regulator on rear axle - Ventilated brake discs - Multi-piece rims, central spider of aluminium alloy, drawn metal channels, front 8,5" × 15, rear 12" × 15 - Tyres, front 225/50 VR 15, rear 345/35 VR 15, all Pirelli P O - Laminated glass windshield - Adjustable steering wheel - Parallelogram windshield wipers - Luggage van capacity 240 liters - 2 light alloy fuel tanks, total capacity 120 liters.

Fahrgestell
Rohrrahmen - Aufbauboden aus Glasfaser - Aluminium u Kompositen-Karosserie - 2-sitziges Coupé - Spur vorne 15 mm, hinten 1606 mm - Radstand 2500 mm - Laenge 41 mm - Breite 2000 mm - Hoehe 1070 mm - Gewicht 14 Kg - Laengsliegender Mittelmotor und Getriebe - Unabha gige Aufhaengung vorne und hinten - Stossdaempfer n coaxialen Federn - Hintere Aufhaengung mit vier Sto daempfern - Kurvenstabilisator vorne und hinten - Glei laufende Achswellen - Zahnstangenlenkung - Zweikrei Bremsen, hydraulisch, mit Servobremse - Bremsregler Hinterachse - Belueftete Bremsscheiben - Felgen zusa mensetzbar, mit Zentral-Stern aus Alu-Legierung, Kana aus gezogenem Metall, vorne 8.5" × 15, hinten 12" × 15 - I fen, vorne 225/50 VR 15 Pirelli P O, hinten 345/35 VR 1 Pirelli P O - Windschutzscheibe aus duennem Verbundgl - hoehen- und tiefenverstellbare Lenksaeule Parallelogramm- Scheibenwischer-Kofferauminhalt 240 Li - Zwei Benzintanks aus Leichtmetall, Gesamtinhalt 120 Li

Brands Hatch Indy Circuit

We were using Brands Hatch's 'Indy' circuit. It was once known more sensibly and modestly as the Club Circuit, but a few years ago they persuaded a few Indianapolis-type CART single-seater racers (though at that time they were still known as USAC cars) to come over to Britain for two races, one at Silverstone and one at Brands. I think they used the Club Circuit at Brands Hatch because the entry was too small to justify using the whole circuit.

Also, I should point out that the names of corners at Brands Hatch have changed over the years. You can tell how old people are according to which set of names they use. In the old days, you went through Paddock Hill Bend, then Druids, then Bottom Bend, and along the Bottom Straight to South Bank. It is here that the Grand Prix Circuit (it's still called that, though, sadly, it seems unlikely that there will ever again be a British Grand Prix in Kent) turns sharp left. For the Club Circuit, we have a faster left-hander, leading to Kidney and Clearways (where the Grand Prix Circuit rejoins us), which leads out on to the Top Straight.

Now you still start with Paddock, one of the world's most challenging bends, fast with a blind apex and a change in camber, leading into a severe dip which bears the scars of several grounded chassis members.

But the rise after that, up to the 180deg Druids hairpin is now known as Hailwood Hill, and the dip afterwards is called Graham Hill, which I am told is an amusing pun. Graham Hill Bend leads into the Cooper Straight, South Bank is now Surtees and Kidney is McLaren, and the second part of Clearways is Clark Curve, leading into the Brabham Straight.

Reluctantly, in deference to the young and ignorant, I'll stick with this second set of names, even though when Clark, Hill, and the others drove there they used the old names.

As I set off on to the circuit, I tried hard to eliminate from my mind the fact that a second-hand Countach was worth at that time approximately double the £109,000 list price of a new one, or at least it would be if I didn't roll into a ball of scrap.

There were problems in driving the Countach at Brands Hatch. Not the least of these was, again, that of all-round visibility. To get through Druids, the hairpin, for example, it is necessary to spend a few seconds looking through the large triangular right front side window. Formula 1 cars have only a *slightly* more minimal view to the rear, but at Brands Hatch I knew there wasn't much likelihood of anyone coming up to catch me unawares.

Once up to speed, I was using third gear for Paddock and holding third until the braking area for Druids, where I'd briefly snatch second. Early in the descent to Graham Hill Bend, I was snicking back into third gear, which would be held all the way along the Cooper Straight and through Surtees, for which it was necessary to brake (in some slightly slower cars – or those with serious downforce – it can be taken flat), and then quite hard braking is necessary after crossing the kerb on the right to line up for Clark Curve. Third gear seemed more advantageous here than second, the engine providing ample torque at low revs, while the time occupied by dropping down a gear (and then changing up again) was compounded by time lost through wheelspin.

Clark Curve is a seriously tricky bend where it's important not to apply too much power too soon. That can push the car to the outside of the road, where a change in camber and loss of grip because of minuscule deposits of tyre debris will all too easily entice the car towards the run-off area if not actually into the tyre barrier. It's also an important bend, as it is followed by the only straight of any significance. I found the gearchange marvellous on the circuit, with no baulking and a very clearly defined gate.

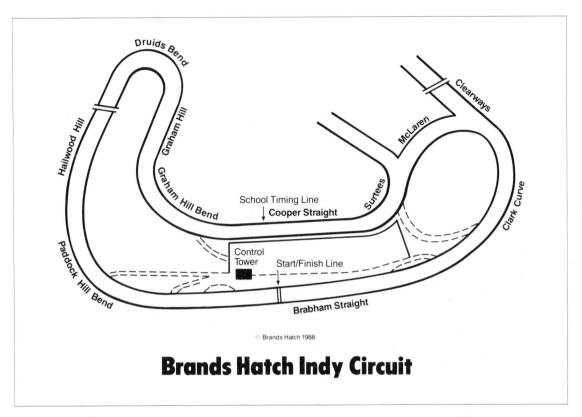

Brands Hatch Indy Circuit

This is the circuit used by the author on his test drive of the Anniversary.

Along the Brabham Straight, I was changing into fourth near the 7,500rpm rev limit, which is a speed of 120mph (193kph). Approximately 130mph (209kph) can be achieved before the necessity to brake conservatively early for Paddock. There is plenty of time along the Brabham Straight to check all the gauges in a Countach (and they are all easily readable, with the exception of the over-fussy speedo), which can lap this undulating 1.2036-mile (2km) circuit in just under 56sec, an average speed of more than 77mph (124kph).

Considering the fact that the Countach is designed as a road car, it performs remarkably well on a racing circuit. There is initial understeer, certainly (and when there isn't in a road car, there is cause for concern), but it is not excessive. Yet, though it seems amazing when the steamroller rear tyres are examined, application of throttle can be used to induce neutrality as the car passes the apex.

I have attempted elsewhere in this book to dispel the myth that a Countach without that ugly rear wing is unstable. Admittedly, the speeds reached on Brands Hatch's Indy circuit are not up in the Jumbo-jet take-off zone, even with this much power on tap, but the car ran straight and true along the Brabham Straight, didn't weave under braking (either before or after the brakes faded), and displayed the reassuring stability which is the hallmark of a well-sorted chassis. The steering too is excellent, giving lots of feedback but with kickback virtually removed.

Above and right: *The author driving a Countach Anniversary on a chilly autumn day at Brands Hatch.*

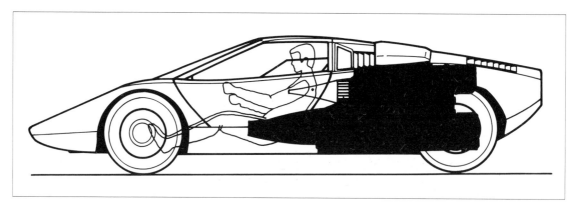

While it is true that the Countach driver sits well forward in the chassis, his feet are still (just) behind the front axle line, an important safety measure.

This photograph was taken as part of the Lamborghini 25th anniversary limited-edition brochure. The catalogue reveals that the Anniversary answers to different names in different parts of the world. In Italy, it is known as the Countach 25°, in Germany as the Jubilaeums Countach, and in France as the Countach 25ème.

The original Lamborghini design with the gearbox mounted ahead of the engine – this is taken from the Lamborghini anniversary brochure.

Though it requires just over three turns to go from one lock to the other, the gearing is such that only just over half a turn is required to negotiate a tight bend like Druids.

With its firm suspension, and centralised masses, there is very little sensation of pitch or squat in the Countach even when braking and accelerating hard. However, squat *can* be detected in an exhilarating fashion when accelerating out of Clark Curve, and the front end feels lighter as the fat rear tyres are squashed down to the tarmac, working hard at delivering all 455bhp.

As is often the case with mid-engined cars, it does not pay to treat the Countach like a toy. It was far easier in the front-engined Lister-Jaguar, for example, to provoke a tail slide and hold it. The Countach could be safely persuaded to tighten its line but if similarly played about with, it would snap out of shape and needed to be caught early to avoid a spin. My shorter but faster colleague Mark Hales found that his difficulty at this point in the proceedings was the simple impossibility of bracing himself within the cockpit.

Although the brakes of a Countach are

perfectly adequate for road use, on a circuit they get more of a pounding, and the 15in (381mm) rims (which all 'supercar' manufacturers used several years ago) do not permit the disc diameters available to those using the more recently favoured 16 and 17in (406 and 432mm) wheels.

After a couple of laps, the Countach's brakes start to fade away – especially the front ones – and in turn this causes the rear ones to lock. After a few rapid laps, it is necessary to cruise gently for two or three circuits in order to allow the pads to cool.

As I mentioned earlier, the Countach is not designed as a racing car. Nevertheless, this brake performance was a bit disappointing. Some owners will want to drive on circuits, perhaps as members of a high-performance car-driving club.

It is possible that on a circuit with longer straights, such as Goodwood, Oulton Park or Donington Park amongst others, the pads would have more opportunity to cool down, although I rather doubt it. Maybe harder pads would solve the problem.

5 What the Magazines Said

From its launch to its demise the Countach was the world's most controversial car. A lot of journalists got into it with the intention of proving all the extravagant claims to be wrong. Those who stepped out, even of the slower versions, were usually impressed; those who drove the faster ones almost always became converts.

LP400

Motor, 1973

One of the first detailed articles about the Countach appeared in *Motor*, 13 October 1973. It was written by the late Pete Coltrin (himself later the co-author of a book about the Countach), who clearly reflected the preoccupations of motoring in 1973. The report's heading tells its own story: 'Countach – last of the supercars?' At that time nobody – motoring journalists or general public – believed that supercars were here to stay. Ray Hutton's article in *Autocar* eight months later carried an identical message, namely that the Countach was the last of the dinosaurs . . .

Had you suggested to anyone then that in the late 1980s both Ferrari and Porsche would be building limited-edition models doing 200mph (322kph), and that not only would Jaguar's V12 still be in production, but that BMW would also build an engine of that size, and that Mercedes-Benz would still be using a big V8 with a capacity of 5.6 litres, you'd have been regarded as mad.

Coltrin, an expatriate American who lived in Modena for many years, was among the best-informed journalists of his time on the Italian motor industry, and that clearly comes through from his article. He knew the people – Stanzani and Wallace, for example – and he was able to provide a vivid picture of early Countach testing, much of which seems extraordinary today: using wool-tuft for final air-flow tests instead of a wind tunnel, for example (a scale model had earlier been tested in a tunnel).

It is interesting to note that the problem of evacuation in an accident had been considered at such an early stage, and at that time the intention was to make the doors removable by pull-ring pins. This plan never went into production, presumably because of the difficulty of meeting safety regulations with such a system.

Certainly, there was a clear vision of the type of buyer at whom the new car was aimed:

'Stanzani said it would be a true *"macchina sportiva stradale"* – neither a GT car nor a race car but a car guaranteed to do, among other things, a standing kilometre in 23 seconds or less. It would combine performance with comfort. Performance here was defined as a high power-to-weight ratio, stability and manoeuvrability. None of these qualities could be neglected, each had to have a well thought-out approach and solution. The car would not be built to a price. As far as was practicable, cost would be no object to achieve the aims although, as

Above: *Note that Gandini's periscope mirror made the transition from prototype to production cars (though it was abandoned with the introduction of the LP400S).*

Left: *This right-hand-drive LP400 from 1975 shows that Britain was recognised early on as an important market for Lamborghini. The owner considered one door mirror sufficient.*

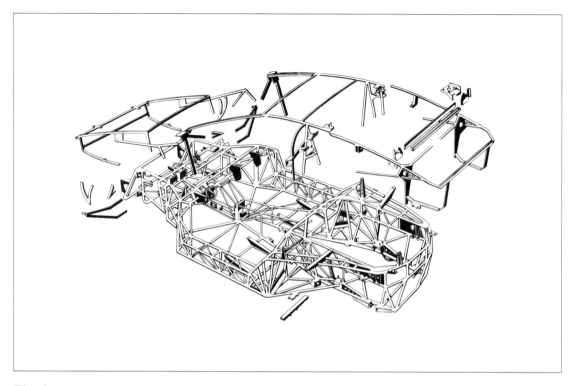

This diagram gives an indication of the intricacy of the Countach's chassis, whose complex of round-section tubes gives it exceptional rigidity.

with all things, the line has finally to be drawn somewhere. The car would be sold only to discerning customers, known to the factory – serious enthusiasts who would appreciate such a car and know how to use it. A prestige car certainly by its very nature, but not for "status symbol" seekers. Too many of the latter gave the Miura a somewhat tarnished reputation – like pop stars who made headlines by crashing as many as three Miuras and others whose lines of "business" didn't exactly enhance the Miura's image.

'The Countach, says Stanzani, is a car for the true enthusiast who will put up with certain inconveniences and do without minor amenities, such as limited luggage space and no electric window-winders (impossible anyway). Provision is made for air conditioning but Lamborghini will be more than happy if no one ever asks for it (the weight penalty and a 10–15bhp penalty make them wince).'

It is no longer regarded as 'impossible' to install electric window-winders to operate a glazed slot a couple of inches high which barely meets the definition of the word 'window': ridiculous perhaps, but not impossible. 'Luxury' items such as air-conditioning were regarded in those days as effete, as well as a nuisance for the production line. In any case, those were the days when the 'ventilation system' in Italian cars was operated by the window-winders. It was not until cars like the Lancia Delta appeared that Italian manufacturers began to fit face-level vents; and it was several years later that they

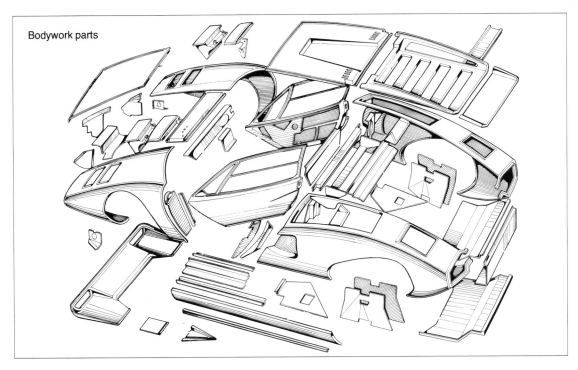

Bodywork parts

For the LP400, there were forty-four body components, most of them
hand-beaten light aluminium. However, even at that time, glass
fibre was used in many concealed areas. Use of composite
materials increased gradually throughout the Countach's
lifespan, though its basic construction was essentially unchanged.

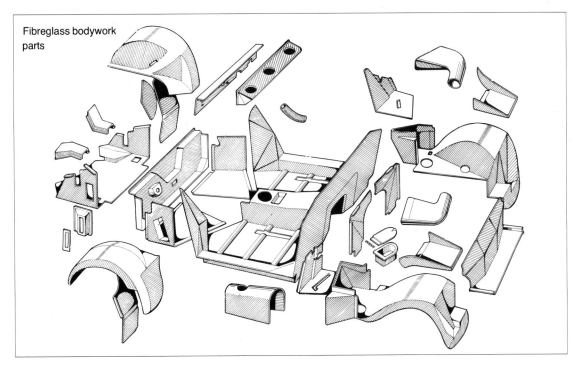

Fibreglass bodywork
parts

learned how to make some air come through them.

Lamborghini's acceleration target of a standing kilometre in under 23sec is very fast indeed by any standards, even today. Then it was quite startling. No Countach before the QV could manage it, though some of them weren't far off, but Stanzani at this stage could not have foreseen, or was not yet admitting, that he would be forced to use an engine with a swept volume one litre smaller than he had originally intended.

According to Coltrin, it was considered that the shortage of skilled craftsmen, rather than demand, would determine the production rate; little did Lamborghini foresee the problems that lay ahead!

Autocar, 1974

Seven months later, when Ray Hutton reported in *Autocar* on his visit to the factory, there was a 100kph or 62mph overall speed limit in Italy, the local response to the world's 'fuel crisis'.

Italians have never taken speed limits very seriously. The Italian government introduced some bizarre limits a few years ago, in which cars with engines of different capacities were theoretically supposed to keep to different limits. Of course, it was a lot of nonsense, and nobody took any notice. But in 1988, things became more serious when a set of limits was introduced, with different maximum speeds allowed according to whether it was a week-day or the weekend. Again this gave the appearance of a self-mocking approach, but on this occasion, cameras were installed along the *autostradas* and several people received summonses for exceeding speed limits. Wealthy Italians – among them several Countach owners – regarded this turn of events as insulting, as well as irritating, and they paid known 'villains' to remove or destroy most of the cameras.

Back in 1974, many Italian drivers treated the 100kph limit with contempt. Even so, it was not an ideal time to launch such a car as the LP400. Once again, the heading to the article made a gloomy prognostic: 'Supercars – the end of the line?' The analysis was that speed limits, tightening legislation and the lack of opportunity to use 180mph (290kph) performance would put paid to cars of this type. The price of the Countach for the UK, just announced, was £16,314. That was quite a lot of money in those days. Bob Wallace, the factory's test driver, could not imagine 'that Lamborghini – or anyone else – would ever build another car of this type'. Yes, it was 1974.

But the Lamborghini people were defiant in adversity, as Hutton, then Editor of *Autocar*, made clear:

'I should have realized that it would take more than an economy-imposed 100kph speed limit to hold down the Italian enthusiasm for fast and beautiful cars. We were rushing through the lanes around Sant' Agata Bolognese. The speedometer flashed up to 220kph. There is a cluster of houses ahead – and a clear road beyond. The acceleration continues, to the accompaniment of the raucous, marvellous noise of a V12 on

full song. The people who live in the out-
skirts of Modena are used to seeing exotic
cars "on test". But this one still makes them
stop in their tracks, smile and wave in
encouragement.'

Even in 1986, I found exactly the same
response in villages around Sant'Agata, and
I suppose it is the same today, though
'Diablo!' is perhaps not such a refreshing
and innocent expletive as 'Countach!'

The article was not a test of the Countach
– indeed, Ray Hutton (like Coltrin) was not
actually permitted to drive the car – but it
provides a useful insight into its development at a crucial, early stage, as by then,
the attempts to develop the 5-litre engine
had been shelved. The Countach's maximum
speed was not yet a controversial subject, so
the following extract is interesting:

'Lamborghini do not yet know what that
maximum speed is, which further under-
lines the difficulty of finding somewhere to
achieve getting on for 200mph in controlled
conditions. Wallace took the second prototype (modified to the mechanical specification of the production car) to Fiat's private
5km stretch of *autostrada* outside Turin and
recorded 290kph (180.2mph) at 7,600rpm in
top. He is sure that given a long enough run-
in it would pull 7,800 so the magic 300kph
(186.4mph) is on the cards, even if 200mph
(the original target of the advertising people,
if not the engineers) is not. Wallace isn't
very interested in top speed now: he is confi-
dent that it can go faster than any customer
is likely to want, and, more important, do it
in safety.'

There is no indication of the type of tyres
fitted to this early example of the LP400, but
it was still running on 15in (229mm) rims,
and also wider at the rear – 9.5 (241) rather
than 9in (229mm) – than the official production version of the car.

At that point in the Countach's develop-

ment, records Hutton: '. . . there has been no
attempt to meet American so-called safety
regulations with this car: the Countach
won't be sold in the United States'. Nor
would there be for a further twelve years,
though several Countaches crossed the
Atlantic before then, skirting American regulations by being classified as 'personal
imports'.

The article ends with a quote from Wallace: 'If this is the last car of its type ever to
be made, we figure we should build it as best
we possibly can . . .'

Motor, 1975

In this test from 1 November 1975, there is a
photograph of two lines of black rubber running parallel for fifty yards – laid down by
the exuberant Rex Greenslade (then one of
Motor's resident testers, and also a skilled
racing driver) in the course of the performance testing at MIRA.

Elsewhere in the article (the first-ever full
test of a Countach) there is a reference to the
tightness of the engine, because the car had
only 373 miles (600km) on the clock. It is
just as well that Lamborghini build their
engines to last.

Rex Greenslade lays some rubber on MIRA's horizontal mile straight, with the Peiseler fifth wheel clamped to the rear of the car. In those days it drove an accurate but bulky electro-mechanical recorder. Today's more compact units are fully electronic.

Though it missed the promised standing-kilometre time by 3sec, this LP400 was not slow off the line by any means, achieving 0–60mph (0–96.5kph) in 5.6sec and 0–100mph (0–161kph) in 13.1sec. But see how sluggish it was in top gear, especially when compared with the LP500S and the 5000QV: 50–70mph (80–110kph) in 12.0sec. This suggests that the engine was not delivering its full performance, particularly in the lower reaches of the rev range. It is evident that the Countach drew respect from *Motor's* testers:

'Lamborghini make one a week and you can count the number sold in this country so far on the fingers of one hand. So it's certainly exclusive. But there are better reasons than that for buying a Countach. True, it is rare and it does have the style, panache and rakish lines that attract fascinated attention. But it is also an extremely well engineered car and perhaps deserves more respect than bestowed on a rich man's toy. Shattering performance allied to excellent handling, roadholding and brakes add up to a formidable package, as well they ought for £17,890.08!'

The price had gone up. It was well above the average cost of a house in those days. There is no reference, anywhere in the test, to any oil crisis (though 10mpg is prefaced by the word 'only'), and there are no gloomy predictions about the imminent end of the world as we know it. How things can change in little more than a year!

ROAD TEST

Reproduced from *Motor*
1 November 1975

Many styling exercises produced for motor shows are impractical, exaggerated machines never intended for production. They're often commissioned for prestige and publicity reasons by large firms to demonstrate the talents of young designers and to see just what can be done when normal constraints are thrown to the wind. If you can't change a plug without removing the engine first or even see out properly because of internal reflections, it is of little consequence.

Surprisingly, a number of these so-called one-offs do get into production. The Lotus Esprit is one, Lamborghini's most exotic and expensive creation yet, the Countach, is another.

Few people gazing at the original Bertone Countach at Geneva in 1971 could have regarded it as anything other than a 'show' car. There were those fold-up doors for a start (how did you get out of it if the car rolled?) and the space-age cockpit with its abysmal rear visibility, not to mention the strange engine/transmission configuration.

Bertone and Lamborghini had mounted the all-alloy V12 engine longitudinally in the chassis, (abandoning the Miura's transverse layout), but with the gearbox at its front in the centre of the car. The drive was taken from the gearbox's secondary shaft by a drop-gear to a propeller shaft running rearwards to the final drive housed in an extension of the cast-alloy sump. The intention was to give better weight distribution and a more positive gearchange than the Miura had, which sounded reasonable enough; but would Lamborghini be able to make this unconventional arrangement work well enough on a production car? It seemed unlikely.

Yet intended for production the Countach (pronounced 'coontash', incidentally) certainly was. Two years were spent testing and developing the design (most effort being put into perfecting the unorthodox power train) and when non-prototype versions appeared at the end of 1973 only a pair of NACA ducts on the car's rear flanks and a couple of radiator cowls on its haunches betrayed externally the many mechanical changes under the skin.

The original cobbled-up semi-monocoque chassis had been replaced by a more conventional (and very much more complex) tubular spaceframe; the ingenious periscope mirror arrangement had been dropped in favour of a more conventional mirror; and the larger 4.8 litre engine was shelved indefinitely. Announced as the world's most expensive and fastest car, as well as being the replacement for the Miura, the Countach had a lot to live up to. . .

. . . For the Countach, the Lamborghini four overhead camshaft V12 engine of 3929cc differs only in details from the unit that used to power the Miura. The special cast elektron sump incorporating the differential housing is one obvious change, as are the double rows of horizontal Weber 45 DCOE carburetters (six in all) that dominate the engine – the Miura had four triple down-draught carburetters. The engine produces 375 bhp (DIN) at 8000 rpm – not much under 100 bhp/litre, a yardstick by which people used to judge full-blooded racing engines not so long ago. Times have changed!

Not surprisingly, the engine thrives on revs. There's little point in using less than 4000 rpm for anything other than gentle cruising on a whiff of throttle; open the throttle suddenly at low rpm and the engine cuts dead. But above 4000 rpm it's another story. The exhaust note deepens perceptibly as the car gathers speed and the engine gets a new lease of life as it passes 6000 rpm, when it develops the characteristic V12 – almost F1-like – scream. The way in which it surges on towards the 8000 rpm red line is most exhilarating, especially as there's no fall-off in power.

As the concessionaires are only planning to import a dozen Countachs this year (that's all the factory will supply) we had to do our performance tests on a brand-new, barely run-in example. This perhaps explains why the engine felt rougher than those of other Lamborghinis we've tried, though what an

example with more than about 600 km on the clock would be like we can't say.

Even so, the acceleration was startling. On MIRA's grippy horizontal straight, doing a racing-style start wasn't easy, for the clutch lacked bite and slipped if the revs dropped. The only solution was to suppress our feelings of mechanical sympathy, wind the motor up to 7000 rpm (perilously close to the limit) and release the clutch as quickly and as sharply as possible. The results, were spectacular. Plumes of tyre smoke, a raucous bellow from the exhausts, a neck-jerking surge of acceleration, black lines 50 yards long (we measured them!) and a 0–60 mph time of 5.6 sec. The first to second gearchange came at 65 mph, the next at 83 mph and after only 13.1 sec from rest the car was doing 100 mph. The quarter mile mark rushed past a fraction later (14.1 sec) and when we'd covered a kilometre (25.2 sec) the Countach was doing over 130 mph.

Fast by any standards, but Lamborghini say that a well run-in example should be even quicker with a standing kilometre time of less than 23 sec.

Lamborghini also claim a top speed of over 190 mph, but needless to say we didn't find a road where we could safely (or legally) confirm the figure. Our car seemed to be struggling at 160 mph – we suspect the new engine was not properly on song – and we'd estimate its top speed to be around 175 mph.

At first sight the enormous fuel tanks (mounted racing-style either side of the passenger compartment and each with a capacity of 13.2 gallons) appear more than adequate. But our Countach only did 10 mpg so you can only travel just over 250 miles between stops. Filling the tanks isn't easy either, for the caps are hidden beneath well-camouflaged flaps inside the NACA ducts on each side of the car: a pump attendant's nightmare.

With the gearbox much closer to the driver than in many conventional mid-engined cars, the lever linkage is shorter and the gearchange benefits considerably from the greater precision that this gives. Like all other Lamborghinis (and Ferraris), the five-speed gear pattern is arranged with first across to the left and back, and there is an external metal gate to guide the lever. Both these features are a little off-putting to start with; first to second is an awkward dog-leg and the metal gate enforces accurate movements of the lever. But with a little acclimatisation (and miles – our car's change freed up noticeably during the test) it becomes quite manageable. It's not a sophisticated gearchange though – it's much too heavy for that – but it is fast and the synchromesh unbeatable. Straight-through changes bring forth some groans and shrieks from the gearbox, however.

Gearbox and transmission noise are loud and disturbing. At high rpm – particularly in third gear – the gearlever chatters, zizzes and transmits far too much whine through to the interior. Covering the open gate with your hand reduces the noise, suggesting that some simple soundproofing would be beneficial.

Apart from the low second gear, the gearbox ratios are well chosen. Maxima in the intermediate gears at 8000 rpm are 65, 83, 115 and 149 mph. Fifth gives the car a long-legged gait of 23.78 mph/1000 rpm, though a slightly lower final drive might be an improvement for the car feels over-geared and relatively sluggish in top, an impression exaggerated by the car's poor flexibility.

From the F1-type Koni dampers to the suspension arms and links, the suspension and steering are fully adjustable, which means that, within limits, you can set up a Countach to handle and ride as you wish. The factory normally adjusts the cars so that they handle as near neutrally as possible. Our car had its front track incorrectly set, though, a fault which made the Countach feel unstable under heavy braking and prone to oversteer when cornered near the limit. On the road, we had no trouble controlling the errant tail when it did step out of line, but within the safe confines of MIRA's test track, where very high cornering speeds are possible, it would have been all too easy to spin the car.

Under more normal conditions the Countach behaves extremely well. The light but high geared steering has good feel and allows the car to be placed with great accuracy. The car handles bumpy surfaces well; there's little kickback from the steering and no grounding – faults which often spoil ultrafast sports cars on country roads. Minimal roll, excellent adhesion and good response to the helm allow the car to be steered through a series of bends quickly and safely.

Heavy braking from high speed provoked slight judder and graunching noises from the discs, but no sign of fade. Although they feel dead and fairly heavy, they coped well with the formidable task of repeatedly pulling the Countach down from speeds of 130 mph to 40 mph or less.

There's a surprising amount of luggage space. The main compartment is behind the engine in the tail – a deep square box that will hold more than enough suitcases for a long weekend. There are also small spaces above and around the spare wheel in the front, and the gaps behind the seats if they're not pushed right back.

Headroom is restricted for anyone over 6 ft tall, but mainly because the steering column is adjustable for length as well as height, the driving position is the best we've yet encountered in a Lamborghini. There's plenty of leg and elbow room and the seats are comfortable and hold you tightly in place on corners.

The pedals take some getting used to as they're offset to the left and the brake pedal goes below the accelerator under heavy braking, making heel and toe changes tricky. But Lamborghini can adjust the pedal positions to suit customers.

Two stalks – one each side of the steering

GENERAL SPECIFICATION

Engine

Cylinders	V12
Capacity	3929 cc (240.0 cu in.)
Bore/stroke	82.0/62.0mm (3.22/2.40 in.)
Cooling	Water
Block	Elektron light alloy
Heads	Elektron light alloy
Valves	Dohc per bank
Valve timing	
inlet opens	42° btdc
inlet closes	70° abcd
exhaust opens	64° bbdc
exhaust closes	40° atdc
Compression	10.5:1
Carburetter	6 Weber twin choke 45 DCOE
Bearing	7 main
Fuel pump	Electric
Max power	375 bhp (DIN) at 8000 rpm
Max torque	268 lb ft (DIN) at 5000 rpm

Transmission

Type	5-speed manual
Clutch	Sdp, diaphragm spring
Internal ratios and mph/1000 rpm	
Top	0.755:1/23.7
4th	0.990:1/18.6
3rd	1.310:1/14.1
2nd	1.769:1/10.4
1st	2.256:1/8.1
Rev	2.134:1
Final drive	4.080:1

Steering

Type	Rack and pinion
Assistance	No
Toe-in	2mm
Camber	0
Castor	5
Kingpin	9°
Rear toe-in	3mm

Body/chassis

Construction	Steel tubular chassis aluminium bodywork
Protection	Primer plus 7 coats of paint

Suspension

Front	Independent by wishbones, coil springs, telescopic dampers, anti-roll bar. Fully adjustable.
Rear	Independent by wishbones, coil springs, telescopic dampers, anti-roll bar. Fully adjustable.

Brakes

Type	Ventilated discs front and rear
Servo	Yes
Circuit	Dual
Rear valve	Yes
Adjustment	Automatic

Wheels

Type	Cast magnesium 7½ J front; 9 J rear
Tyres	Michelin XWX: 205/70VR14 front; 215/70VR14 rear
Pressures	35.5 psi front; 43 psi rear

Electrical

Battery	12v, 66 Ah
Polarity	Negative
Generator	70A alternator
Fuses	16
Headlights	455W QI

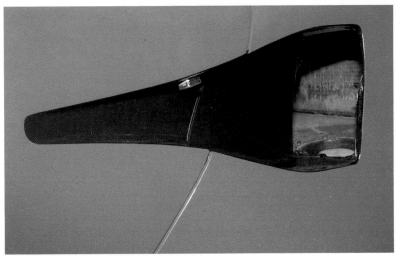

column – incorporate most of the minor switchgear (wash/wipe, headlamp, flash/dip indicators) and are within fingertip reach. The seat belts, however, are awful, difficult to adjust and untidy when not in use.

Seeing out is a good deal easier than the space-age styling suggests from outside. You sit well forward and the nose dips sharply out of sight, which can be a problem when parking. The rear three-quarter view is completely obscured, but you soon learn to adapt to this by approaching road junctions at right angles, as in a van, and looking through the side window. The mirror view aft is quite adequate.

Internal reflections on the windscreen – so often a problem with steeply raked screens – aren't too apparent, but any form of road film is; it pays to keep the windscreen washer well topped up and to use it often.

The interior is tastefully furnished in typical Italian style – matt black velvet-covered facia and polished aluminium surround for the instruments – and is well finished. Stray reflections in day-light spoil what is otherwise an attractive and effective instrument layout (sloping glasses are needed here).

With only the oil radiator mounted forward of the passenger compartment the air conditioning isn't worked so hard as on many more conventional cars as hot air isn't flowing rearwards from the water radiators. In all but the hottest weather it wasn't needed, but when called upon to do so it releases a strong blast of cold air.

The Countach is certainly a very impressive machine. Even allowing for the below-par engine, the Countach compares well with its rivals and sets standards than on the whole are commensurate with its £18,000 price tag. For a show car turned road car, and considering its futuristic styling, it's a good deal more practical than we expected.

How do you get out of it if it rolls? You push the windscreen out!

PERFORMANCE

Maximum Speeds

Speed in gears (at 8000 rpm)

	mph
1st	65
2nd	83
3rd	115
4th	149

Acceleration from rest

mph	sec
0–30	2.7
0–40	3.4
0–50	4.4
0–60	5.6
0–70	7.5
0–80	9.0
0–90	11.1
0–100	13.1
0–110	15.9
0–120	20.3
Standing ¼	14.1
Standing km	25.2

Acceleration in top

mph	sec
50–70	12.0
60–80	12.6
70–90	10.3
80–100	11.0
90–110	11.4
100–120	13.7

Car and Driver, 1975

At about the same time that the test in *Motor* appeared, the American magazine *Car and Driver* ran a wittily sceptical article by Don Sherman (later to be Editor of that same magazine), who clearly put himself outside the circle of believers. At that stage, the Countach was not officially certified for use in the USA, and had to be 'personally imported'.

Sherman's thinly-veiled sarcasm leaves little doubt about his view of the car, and there are some memorable passages in this article:

'More expensive automobiles exist, but you could ride through life in a Countach without ever seeing them.' . . . And:

'Those of us used to buying and driving normal automotive fare, with the thought of a Porsche or maybe a Jaguar as a special treat some day, could never handle the true meaning of a Countach. For its premium price, it should meet or exceed all the abilities of lesser automobiles with ease: it should be as smooth as a Mazda, accelerate faster than a Turbo Carrera, be screwed together better than a Mercedes, handle more gracefully than a Lotus, ride like a Silver Shadow and be more reliable than a Chevy six. The Countach does none of the above. What it does . . . is radiate an air of exclusivity, go incredibly fast in a straight line, look good in any setting and make loud noises.'

But Don Sherman, as well as being a witty writer (he wrote an excellent column in *Car and Driver* magazine for many years) is also rigorously fair in assessing cars. He made it clear that he never had the opportunity to push the Countach to its limits, and gives it the benefit of the doubt when imagining what it *might* be like in those circumstances:

'So where does it all come together? Probably when you blast past the California Highway Patrol pace cruisers who manage the LA–Vegas corridor like hall monitors and live to tell your friends about it without going to jail. And probably at such speeds engineer Dallara has all the physics worked out to actually make the Countach fun to drive. Perhaps at 150mph aerodynamic downforce loosens up the high-friction steering, the ventilation begins to flow and you don't have to worry about sightseers who insist on touching. Somewhere the Countach must reach its stride. But the dues are high to find out if and where.'

Road & Track, 1976

It's a pity that the *Road & Track* test of February 1976 contains no figures for acceleration in fourth and top gears, to compare with those in *Motor* the previous autumn.

The standing-start times aren't as good as *Motor*'s, with the car a full second slower to 30mph (48kph) from rest, a margin which persists at 60mph (96.5kph), and which has spread to 2sec by 120mph (193kph). The reasons for this are explained in rather haughty detail in the text:

'Our English cousins at *Motor* recently tested a Countach and by suppressing their feelings of mechanical sympathy, winding the engine up to 7000rpm and releasing the clutch as sharply as possible achieved some spectacular results, including two black lines 50 yards long, a 0–60mph time of 5.6sec and a quarter-mile time of 14.1sec. In deference to the almost irreplaceable nature of the car (and to the owner who was standing nearby), we opted for a less auspicious and safer technique . . .'

It is quite extraordinary how the presence of a car's owner can induce in a road tester his normally suppressed 'feelings of mechanical sympathy'.

The differences in the figures are interesting in that they illustrate what can be gained by using a brutal, racing-style start. Conversely, *Motor* was more cautious in its estimate of the car's top speed (though I return to the strong impression that the car tested in England was down on power).

LP400S

Car, 1978

The Australian Mel Nichols is one of the characters of British motoring journalism.

He was possibly the most imaginative Editor of *Car*, and he invented a new genre of driving impression: this was conducted from the passenger seat and extended into a full-length test. It was so skilfully done that often it was impossible to tell that he hadn't actually driven the car himself. Even today there is no one who can perform that task with such impressive confidence.

Try not to inhale too deeply:

'The straight was running out and we were rushing at the bend. Stanislao Sterzel's foot stayed flat to the foor and the V12 behind our heads – almost *between* our heads – went on snarling. The tachometer needle went on climbing: six-six . . . six-seven . . . six-eight. Even at those revs, in fifth, and thus with the speed already well in excess of 170mph, we were still being pressed back hard into our seats, prisoners of that incredible powerplant. Such harnessed savagery! Such thrust! Would it ever stop? Was it running away with us sweeping us beyond control as surely as though we were in the clutches of a rip-tide?'

It is difficult to know exactly what to make of the estimates of top speed given here by Nichols. Having caught his breath after recovering from all that thrust, he estimates that Sterzel took him through a bend at 184mph (296kph) and went on to pull 194mph (312kph) at 7,500rpm.

We can only hazard a guess at the specification of this 'development car', in particular its power output and gearing. Certainly, the production version of the LP400S, which appeared shortly afterwards, was substantially slower than suggested here, and was in fact the slowest of all Countach models, thanks to its combination of poor aerodynamic efficiency and relatively low power. At 7,500rpm it would be doing 184 (296), not 194mph (312kph).

This test appeared during Lamborghini's darkest hours, when the company was struggling to survive, the 'management' rarely to be seen, and the production line constantly in danger of enforced rest periods because of the absence of components. Dallara was clearly in evidence at the time, but whatever happened to Franco Baraldini (then a resident engineer), Fiorenzo Forini (Chief Experimental Engineer) and Stanislao Sterzel ('one of Europe's more promising racing drivers')? Presumably, they all left, disliking the irregularity of arrival of their pay packets. It is extraordinary that *anyone* stayed.

Road & Track, 1978

In December of that year, *Road & Track* magazine published the first US road test of the LP400S, under the title: 'Still the ultimate exotic?' Presumably, by 'exotic' they meant 'exciting' or 'dramatic', rather than simply foreign, and 'ultimate' does not mean 'last'.

This LP400S was in full Federalised emissions specification, fitted with catalytic converters, smaller carburettors, and so on. So the acceleration in those circumstances is quite impressive, though the 0–100mph (0–161kph) time (14.4sec) is a couple of blinks slower than in the previous test of the LP400 (trickled away from rest, but not strangled by emissions equipment). Clearly, there was no private owner nervously observing the test on this occasion, because you would not achieve 0–60mph (0–96.5kph) in 5.9sec in a Countach by gently easing off the line. Once again there are no single-gear acceleration figures.

Road & Track makes a sober (and probably accurate) assessment of the Federalised car's maximum speed potential:

'Our estimate is that the Countach S in de-smogged trim would top out at 7,500rpm in 5th gear, which translates to *only* 164mph, compared to 175mph for the S without emission controls.'

LP500S

Autocar, 1982

This test is of one of the first LP500S models, introduced in 1982.

The in-gear acceleration figures suggest a slightly different torque curve from that of the car tested by *Motor* eighteen months later. It is worth noting that *Motor's* car was fitted with the rear wing, while this one, driven by *Autocar* in Italy, was not. However, it seems more likely that the difference resulted from the significant changes in engine response that can result from a relatively small change in tune when you've got six twin-choke carburettors. Whichever is the case, although *Autocar's*

standing-start times look impressive, and the best published up to that point in an English-language magazine, they are no match for *Motor's*. Nevertheless, this car clearly had a healthy, if rather new and tight, engine, and it is interesting to note that it ran out of breath at only 6,700rpm in fifth gear, corresponding to 164mph (264kph).

Car and Driver, 1983

The first time *Car and Driver* subjected a Countach to performance tests was in December 1983. The model was called the LP5000S in the USA, what Europeans knew as the LP500S. (In America, they often add an extra nought just to give the product a little more *identity*.)

Patrick Bedard, another one-time Editor, and one of numerous people of great talent

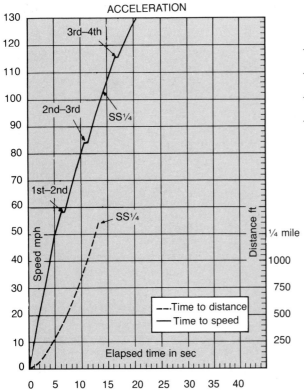

LP500S

LP400

Above, left and below: *The Countach on its home ground. This is the 5000* quattrovalvole *with which we achieved the performance figures for* Fast Lane *in 1986.*

Left: *A discreet car and a modest little place in the country: 1981 Countach LP500S.*

(for both writing and driving) to have worked for *Car and Driver* over the years, expressed his doubts early in this test, which was sub-titled 'Life in the whips-and-chains lane': 'This is a bad boy's car, and everybody knows it . . . Just being seen at the wheel of such a thing is prima facie evidence that you're a regular traveller beyond the borders of good judgment, good sense and good taste.'

Bedard exposes Lamborghini's extravagant top-speed claims, which were only vindicated by the arrival of the 5000 (here we're talking in Italian thousands) *quattrovalvole*, and his observations on the rear aerofoil are apt:

'Bad boys are always claiming to have the Fastest Car. This is an argument we are unable to settle for the time being, but we do have some significant observations on top speed. Although the US importer has certified the Countach and plans to bring in at least 75 per year starting in January, there were no certified examples ready in time for our testing. Our driving was done in a six-Weber European-specification car rated at 368hp at 7,500rpm; the US version is said to have a torque curve at least as strong, but its power trails off above 6,000rpm to a peak of 348hp. In any case, the Euro version maxed out at 150mph – fast, but certainly not out of the range of Boxers and good running 930 Porsches*. Unbolting the optional (at $5,500) wing from the rear increased speed to 160mph with only a very minor loss in directional stability. Not ordering the wing has to be the cheapest speed secret in the world.'

Bedard finishes with another droll remark: 'It's not what the Countach can do for you that counts, but what it does *to* others. This car was made for shattering sensibilities. It performs equally well in heavy-duty neighbourhood work or on fleeting targets of

opportunity. If driving it requires earplugs and the strength of two legs on the clutch, well, nobody ever said being a bad boy was all fun.'

But did he really *like* it?

Motor, 1984

Motor set some new records with the Countach LP500S it tested in its issue of 17 March 1984, such as 0–60mph (0–96.5kph) in under 5sec.

The car used for the test belonged to Barry Robinson who has been a Countach fan for many years, and has owned several. He's always been generous in lending his car for testing purposes to selected journalists, and this example was neither the first nor the last Countach to carry the familiar registration 'BR 33'.

This car's standing-start figures were substantially better than those recorded nine years earlier in the LP400, but – more significantly – the fifth and fourth gear figures are also now more than respectable – even if still quite a way short of those of the 5000QV.

This LP500S has the big wing on the tail, which some people like. The top speed, recorded at Millbrook's two-mile banked circular track, was 155.1mph (249.5kph). Such is the variation in the effect of tyre scrub on cars at Millbrook that it is impossible to judge how much of the failure of the car to go faster was due to the wing, and how much to the banked circuit. The road test writer probably judged it well, suggesting that this would translate into 160mph (257kph) on a flat surface, and perhaps as much as 175mph (281.5kph) with the wing removed. But that is quite a lot faster than *Autocar* had achieved two years earlier . . . There always seem to be a lot of 'ifs' and 'buts' and 'however's' in relation to the maximum speed of the Countach.

The road test begins with a few remarks about the car's image and appearance, and

*The 911 Turbo in Europe.

the effect it has on passers-by; but ends by almost pleading people to buy the car for its intrinsic engineering merits: 'Beyond the charisma and beneath the dream-car shape, there's a car of real substance and ability which, by our figures, is the ultimate production car. If you want to, and you can afford it, buy a Countach as a car to be seen in; but if you've got the driving skill and the automotive appreciation, buy it for what it is.'

Car, 1984

Barry Robinson's LP500S made another appearance in the same month, this time in *Car* magazine, in a group test with the Ferrari Boxer (then nearing the end of its era), Aston Martin Vantage, and Porsche 911 Turbo.

Steve Cropley, a highly professional journalist who was then the Editor of *Car*, carefully explains in his 'Finding out' article at the end of the test, that 'we never resorted to a tape measure and minimally to our timing gear', adding that *Car*'s 'doughty test team' took the rather lofty view that such things didn't really matter very much. Things have changed a lot since then, and I think that the test figures published in *Car* these days are more credible.

As far as I know, *Car*'s test equipment at that time was no more elaborate than a couple of stopwatches and a guessometer. But aside from that, if such things don't matter, why did *Car* bother to publish figures at all? Then there is the question of the origin of the figures, which is unexplained. We needn't go into that here.

In fact, the acceleration figures published prove that such things *do* matter, to the extent that if you are going to publish figures at all, you *must* obtain them with the best possible equipment. That includes electronic (or in those days, possibly electromechanical) calculating devices in association either with a fifth wheel, a hub attachment or a sophisticated light-beam system, and an experienced, scientifically ruthless, yet (preferably), mechanically-sympathetic test driver.

Otherwise, you end up with figures like those published in *Car*, which do no justice to the Countach at that stage of its development: 0–60mph (0–96.5kph) in 5.7sec, 0–100mph (0–161kph) in 13.3. Remember that this is the same car which appeared in *Motor* approximately one week after this 'April' edition of *Car* (monthlies are published in the month preceding their cover dates), annihilating those figures, with times of 4.8 and 11.3sec.

Not only do *Car*'s performance figures make the Lamborghini seem substantially slower than it really is, but they are also robbed of significance by the absence of acceleration times in fourth and fifth gears, which provide a great deal of information about the overall performance of a car. The lofty remark that '20–40mph times in top gear don't matter a jot' would not appear in *Car* today.

Having been severely critical, I must add that the test itself is well written and admirably clarifies the strengths and weaknesses of all the cars. In fairness to Aston Martin, it should be pointed out in mitigation that at that point the Vantage was at its worst, on huge Pirelli P7s which did not suit its chassis at all. The writer is perhaps unduly kind about the behaviour of the car on these tyres; it seems that the weather was dry, though, otherwise there would have been further criticisms concerning unpredictable aquaplaning. Earlier versions of the Vantage ran on Pirelli Cinturato CN36 tyres which gave less grip but much more manageable handling, while later ones, with the suspension beautifully tuned to match the characteristics of the excellent Goodyear Eagles, were better in every respect.

The conclusion of the test is well put, and similar to that which has been reached by several writers over the years: 'For sheer

Details of a 1989
quattrovalvole.

Light colours suit few cars, and the Countach is no exception. Otherwise, though, this is the Countach in its finest form, a quattrovalvole *in European specification, ready to leave the factory in 1988.*

outlandish eye appeal, and track-car capability that's translatable for the road, there is simply no better car. It's hard, also, to imagine a better one coming along.'

5000QV

Autocar, 1985

This test (29 May 1985) was the first of the 5000QV to appear in a British magazine, and it was carried out by Michael Scarlett, then *Autocar's* Technical Editor, in Italy.

Slight tightness of the relatively new engine is probably the reason why the performance figures are not quite as good as those recorded by *Fast Lane* the following year. It is interesting that they are almost uniformly slower, for standing-start acceleration, fifth and fourth gears, and top speed. The latter is particularly interesting. The mean speed recorded, 178mph (286kph), is fast, but 5mph (8kph) below that achieved under official scrutiny by the factory at Nardo, and 3mph (5kph) short of the then claimed (and later verified) maximum of Ferrari's Testarossa.

Top speed, where the engine is working hard against aerodynamic factors, and in the Countach still short of its peak power but at a point where the torque curve is threatening to drop away, is more likely to be affected by the tightness of a new engine than is the case with standing-start acceleration. The writer has omitted to mention – he probably forgot under the pressure of producing a test in time for the weekly publication – that this Countach comes minus the big rear wing. But it is interesting that he refers to the 'ideal' straight-line stability at high speed.

Once again, the conclusion of the road-test writer is broadly favourable. Many of the journalists who have tested the Countach have approached it with some scepticism, but virtually all have been won over by its combination of peculiar charm and impressive engineering: 'Bearing in mind that no one buys a car like this for normal reasons, the *quattrovalvole* Countach is presently the supercar to beat.'

Car and Driver, 1986

This was the first test of a Countach which had been certified for use in the United States, rather than imported privately.

Once again the *Car and Driver* writer, in this case Rich Ceppos, give it his all: 'Well, here it is again, folks: the face that broke a million hearts. The four-wheeled pancake that's glamorized every car-mag cover in the western world. The road-sucking Hoover that's vacuum-cleaned countless fantasy highways and ignited endless rumors but, to this day, remains clouded in mystery and myth. Say "Happy Birthday" to the

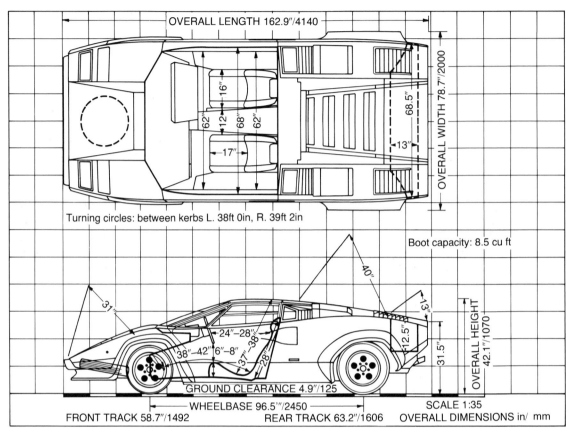

Will it fit your garage? If not, build a new garage. If you can't get planning permission, move house. Though wide at 78.7in (2m), the Countach (this is the quattrovalvole*) is not especially long: at 162.9in (4m), it's nearly 14in (355mm) shorter than a Testarossa, and almost 5in (127mm) shorter than a 328.*

Lamborghini Countach. It turns fifteen this year.' It was the Countach's fifteenth birthday if you consider its 'birth' to have taken place in 1971. Perhaps that was more like its conception, but let's not quibble over details.

Once again here, the maximum speed debate is the dominant focus, and Ceppos makes the rather complicated issues involved very clear. He is unable to resist having a bit of fun here: 'When the question and answer starts, the Countach's pulsating presence is on your side. If you tell the uninitiated that it will do 200mph, they'll believe you. A few might even swallow 215.' Even so, he doesn't state just how fast he believes the car might have gone if it had been running perfectly (it appears to have been down on power), so once again there is frustration, mystery and confusion.

On this occasion, *Car and Driver* drove two cars, one the carburettored, European-specification version, the other a 'Federalised' car with fuel injection. It was the latter's acceleration figures which were published, with 0–60mph (0–96.5kph) in 5.1sec and 0–'100mph (0–161kph) in 11.0; the European model's 0–60mph (0–96.5kph) figure, for comparison, was 4.5sec.

Having been fairly complimentary about the handling (though he does point out that, simply because of its nimbleness, a Toyota MR2 would give it some problems on twisting roads), Ceppos turns to the subject of top speed. The debate ended in this way:

'The Countach is meant to suck the dotted lines off an *autostrada*, not to play boy-Fangio on a narrow back road. You want to know about the speed – the dust and the glory and the banshee wail. Is the Countach the one or isn't it?

'We held the pedal of the European model down until kingdom come and found our test car's limit at 7,000rpm, 500 short of the red line. The engine flattened out noticeably at high rpm, and we doubt very much that all

449 horses were present and accounted for. Our computations point to more like 370.'

However, Ceppos mentions that this car, which managed 166mph (267kph), was fitted with 'the optional $4,000 rear wing in place'. He continues: 'Without it (the wing), our somewhat sickly European car should have climbed easily to 175 or 180mph. That makes the factory's claim of 173mph for the American model (sans wing) quite believable.'

A Countach only has to be a fraction out of tune to let itself down in that area of mystical significance (if minor importance in the 'real world') – maximum speed. Even without the wing, it has a large frontal area to push through the wind, and when you are up over 170mph (273.5kph) a few missing horsepower can make a disproportionate difference.

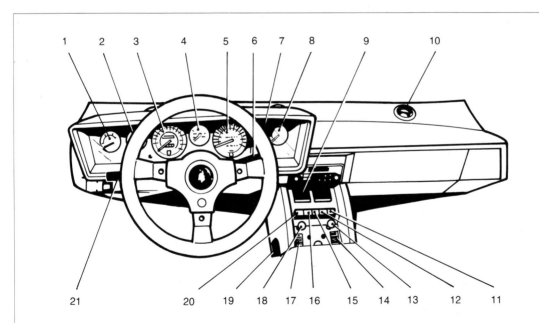

1 Battery volts, **2** Oil temperature, **3** Speedometer, **4** Oil pressure **5** Rev counter, **6** Wipe/Wash stalk, **7** Water termperature, **8** Fuel level, **9** Air cond. outlet, **10** Demist outlet, **11** Heater fan, **12** Fog lamp, **13** Air cond. control, **14** Demist control, **15** Hazard flasher, **16** Headlamp lift, **17** Water valve control, **18** Air cond. fan, **19** Handbrake, **20** Sidelamps, **21** Sidelamps, **21** Indicator/horn/dip stalk.

Facia layout of the 5000 quattrovalvole.

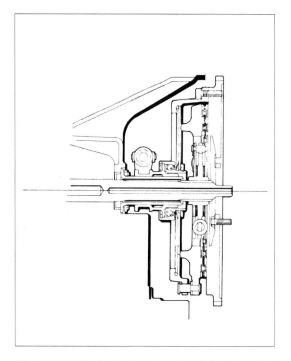 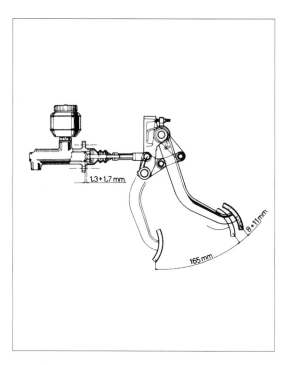

The 5000QV's single dry-plate clutch is hydraulically operated, the pedal acting directly on to the servo. Left: *the clutch control lever.* Right: *clutch and clutch pedal.*

Whatever else his feelings, there can be no doubting the enjoyment enthusiastic driver Rich Ceppos derived from the Countach's V12 engine.

(Incidentally, I'm not sure what a 'Wendy's single' is – Ceppos remarks: 'The split door glass rolls down only enough to slip a Wendy's single through' – but believe it to be a 'fast food' product rather than an undergarment.)

In case you are interested, *Car & Driver's* testers achieved 8mpg overall with the European version of the car. They also took some internal sound readings, recording 63dBA at idle (that's moderately loud), 85dBA cruising at 70mph (112.6kph) (that's *very* loud and 95dBA at full throttle (that's *very loud indeed*).

Road & Track, 1986

Here is an interesting analysis:

'The Countach is its own benchmark, a car that exists outside the constraints of convention, fashion – some may add, taste. But whatever your final estimate of it, one fact remains that after all these years, practically the only clue to the still-stunning Countach's advanced age arises from actually driving it.

'However, after only a short drive, it's abundantly clear – this car has seen many birthdays. Good as it is, and in numerous respects it's very, very good, its keynotes point unmistakably to a time when muscle was everything. This impression arises not simply from consideration of the engine department, awesome as that is, but from the car's dynamic behaviour, the feel of its controls, its entire automotive personality. The Countach is perhaps the last and highest street-legal expression of an era when a supercar's performance was measured against the standard of the Porsche 917, the Ferrari 512, the big-block Can-Am car. Cubic capacity was the answer, efficiency was a footnote, gross weight wasn't even part of the question. In the Countach that formula continues unchanged to the present day. Unquestionably this car is a throwback, though a throwback to an era warmly remembered by anyone lucky enough to have had hands-on experience with the super-fast cars of that time.'

(The (anonymous) writer is trying hard to persuade himself that he's grown up and become responsible, but he can vividly remember the days when he used to have a really good time.) He continues:

'Its mission is not, and never has been, to present a responsible face to the world. Nor is its mission to fine-hone the cutting edge of automotive technology. This is not transportation, in any normal sense. It doesn't even offer "Grand Touring", in any normal sense. It's short on comfort, short on grace, short on ease of operation – indeed, after only the briefest exposure to this car it becomes all too clear that with the Countach, Lamborghini has very successfully avoided overindulging in technological and ergonomic soul-searching. They'll leave that to Ferrari and the Germans.'

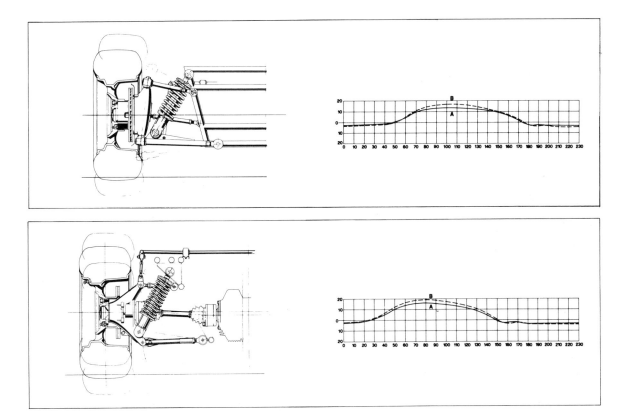

Bump and rebound settings for the front (upper) and rear (lower) dampers of the Countach.

'. . . And if you think that looks good, wait until we remove the packaging.' In order to get around US legislation, ridiculously ugly apendages had to be added to the front and rear of the Countach. This is a 1988 quattrovalvole.

You see, he's beginning to like it, or at least beginning to admit to himself that he liked it all along.

Fast Lane, 1986

If we regard *Car and Driver*'s acceleration figures as definitive for the US-specification Countach with its Bosch K-jetronic injection and no fewer than four catalytic converters (no wonder it costs so much there), then I believe this test contains *the* definitive European figures. Before you claim that I'm blowing my own trumpet, I hasten to point out that although I drove this car and wrote the test, it was Valentino Balboni, the factory's test driver, who executed the acceleration figures; I merely attached the fifth wheel and sat in the passenger seat to operate the telemetry equipment.

As for the question of top speed, that is covered in a separate chapter . . .

<table>
<tr><td>ROAD TEST
Countach QV5000S</td></tr>
<tr><td>Reproduced from Fast Lane
September 1986</td></tr>
</table>

We were wrong and are very happy, ecstatic even, to admit it. Previously exaggerated performance boasts from Lamborghini had deceived us into doubting the 190mph plus top speed claimed for the latest *quattrovalvole* Countach. The truth, however, is that the QV5000S Countach is potentially a 200mph production road car and, as Peter Dron discovered in Italy, it is also the most charismatic and rewarding of all supercars.

Forget the suggestion that it is 'unstable' at high speed without the monstrous rear wing. Ignore those who claim that the Testarossa's 181mph makes it the world's quickest production car. The Countach is the King of Supercars, and nothing else even comes close.

We arrived at the factory at Sant'Agata Bolognese early one morning. It was explained that although we would be allowed to drive the car later in the day, for insurance reasons it was necessary for a 'test driver' to be behind the wheel for the maximum speed runs, to be carried out on the autostrada.

'My name is Piero', said the test driver. 'How do you do?'

We set off down the road. We approach a tightish left-hander, still accelerating fast. Is this to be another of those famous Italian test drivers, with a high ratio of bravery to imagination, and with insufficient skill to make up the difference? We brake late, turn in smoothly with plenty of throttle in second gear. No dramas, just fast and neat.

The same through the next S-bend. This man is good. He always reduces speed in the villages: what you find in this area of industrial/agricultural northern Italy – the entirely flat Emilian Plain – is a demanding

It sounds beautiful, it looks magnificent, and it has few equals for performance: Lamborghini's V12 may become more efficient in future, but it will never be more fun to use than when it had six twin-choke carburettors feeding it.

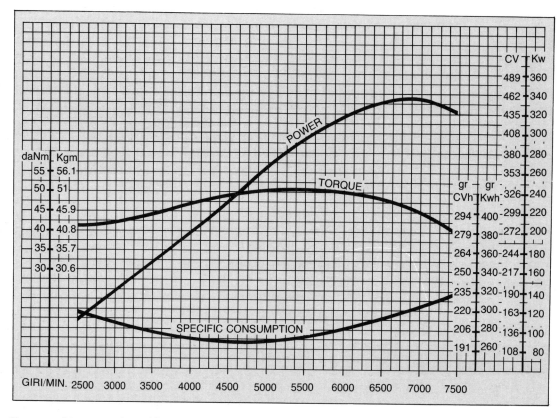

Power and torque and specific consumption curves of the quattrovalvole. The factory, which had in previous years been over-optimistic in its claims, specified 455bhp for the engine fitted with carburettors, but it was generally reckoned to be the minimum figure, and many produced more than that.

stretch of bending road, followed by a village, then another twisty section, then a village, and so on. Even so, as we burble past the houses in those deliciously fading shades of red and cream, people stop whatever they are doing and stare. The Countach may be built only a mile or two down the road, and they must have seen dozens, perhaps hundreds, since the Countach prototype was built 15 years ago. Still the jaw drops and the word forms on the lips: 'Countach!' It's alleged to be what Nuccio Bertone said when he first saw Gandini's design on the drawing board. Roughly and politely, translated, it means: 'Bloody hell, look at that!'

'Have you done any motor racing?' It seems a reasonable question to ask a test driver.

'I won a Formula 3000 race last Sunday . . .'

Hmmm. Formula 3000 is Big Time motor racing, with Cosworth V8 engines; they have fields of about 30 cars and the gap between the front row and the back row is often under two seconds. This man must be very good, because he also won the next race.

'What did you say your name was?'

'Martini.' This is Pierluigi Martini, who comes from a wealthy family, several of *whom have raced. He seems to be the best of them. Having raced a fourth-rate Grand Prix car last year (the Minardi) he decided to switch to something in which he could enjoy himself and stand a chance of winning.*

Lamborghini sells Countaches at a special discount to Grand Prix drivers, and that's one reason why Pierluigi, or Piero as he prefers to be called, has one. Rosberg's pearl white car with big tail wing is at the factory for a service. Martini's car does not have the wing: neither he nor Lamborghini approves of it.

Martini talks of regularly having seen 320kph (roughly one digit short of 200mph) on his speedometer, even at night. The pop-up headlights, he claims, make very little difference to the drag factor. Once, he says, the reading was 325.

This is the sort of wild, fanciful stuff we have heard about the QV5000S for some time. Frankly it is hard to believe, but if we can find a break in the traffic, we'll put it to the test.

The trouble is, Italian motorways have marker posts every kilometre, with no half-kilometre signs. This is fine for the ordinary motorist, but it means that if you are doing a timed high speed run, realistically you need to reach maximum revs about 5sec before the first post, and hold it all the way through to the second one. This is an elapsed time of something like 20sec at maximum speed, and at the sort of speed being considered here, it is a problem, especially with a very definite need to leave a bit of space for braking at the end of the exercise if there is traffic around. It's a pity that the Nardo test track is so far to the south, though that apparently scrubs a few mph off the maximum.

In our ignorance of the Countach, we not only disbelieved the performance claims for it, but we also believed that myth about the car being unstable at high speed without the wing fitted. That may perhaps have been true of earlier versions, but it certainly

doesn't apply to the Quattrovalvole 5000S which runs arrow-straight at its maximum speed. There was a tendency for the front end to become light, but a small but significant change in both the overall ride height and in the attitude of the car (it is now pitched ever so slightly forwards) has altered that. But even Martini's Countach, built before these changes were introduced, did not wander as we flew along the tarmac at a speed approaching that at which a Boeing 747 takes off.

We turn off on to a different autostrada. At last we get a time – 12.3sec – but the car is still accelerating for at least two thirds of the distance. A check with the calculator reveals that that represents 292.7kph, or 181.9mph. Well, that's seen off the Testarossa, if only by a blink of an eye. We try again and again, but each time we are baulked as the inevitable man in the little Fiat pulls out to pass a truck, all the while almost facing his lady passenger. It seems they are unable to talk without looking at each other.

Finally, we turn on to yet another autostrada. It's clear, and the rev needle is flickering wildly just inside the red sector, and the speedometer reading 320kph. This is it. We pass the first kilometre post. Those tiny specks in the far distance are beginning to be identifiable shapes. Soon, though they would not be aware of it even if they used their rear-view mirrors, they could become a braking area. Click! We pass the second kilometre post, and Piero is safely, very firmly on the brakes to haul us down to traffic speed. We have covered a flying kilometre in 11.46sec, which is 314.1kph metric, 195.2mph Imperial, and bloody quick in anyone's language. Countach!

This is not the end of this section of the job, however; because we are scrupulous about such things, it is necessary to time the car in the opposite direction, too, in order to eliminate factors such as wind speed and direction, and gradient. As far as the latter

A fine example of a 5000 quattrovalvole.

is concerned, the Emilian Plain is like Essex, where molehills are considered to be major topographical features.

On the way back we covered the kilometre in 12.1sec, which means 297kph, 184.9mph. I still feel a bit disappointed with this, because the car may have had a tiny bit left to come, but even so it works out at a mean speed of 305.8kph and 190.1mph. That may be 1mph faster or slower than the Ferrari GTO, but either way it doesn't matter too much. It's possible that the Porsche 959 is a few mph faster, and it seems that Aston's Zagato is not far behind.

Unlike the other cars mentioned, the Countach is a production car, even if it is hardly in the volume business. More than 1,000 Countaches have been built since the first LP400 appeared in 1973. There was one prototype, called the LP500, before that. It was intended to have a 4,971cc engine producing 440bhp at 7,400rpm, and 366lb ft of torque at 5,000rpm. Top speed, it was hoped, would be 186mph.

The LP400 was in production for five years, and 150 were built. Its engine was smaller – 3,929cc (with a narrower bore and shorter stroke), and it produced 375bhp at 8,000rpm and 266lb ft of torque at 5,000rpm. Maximum speed was reckoned to be about 175mph, with 0–60mph in around 5.5sec.

In 1978, the LP400S appeared, with 353bhp at 7,500rpm and 267lb ft of torque at 5,000rpm, with the same swept volume. The factory claimed a maximum of 'more than 186mph'. It was at that time that the number of 'Doubting Thomases' regarding Lamborghini's performance claims increased dramatically. A further power and torque boost (to 375bhp/7,000rpm and 302lb ft/4,500rpm) was achieved in 1982 when the LP500S was introduced with the present model's 85.5mm bore, and a stroke of 69mm, giving a capacity of 4,754cc. Curiously, the factory revised its top speed claim downwards to 'more than 180mph', which was a bit more credible, and may even have been true.

But it was last year that the King of the Countaches, the Quattrovalvole 5000S, took its bow. Until this point, the Countach had always had two camshafts above each bank of six cylinders, but now for the first time it was supplied with four valves per cylinder, a total of 48. At the same time the stroke was stretched to 75mm, and the six downdraught twin-choke Webers changed from 45 DCOE to 44 DCNF. Power went up to a massive yet nominal 455bhp at 7,000rpm and torque to 369lb ft at 5,200rpm. Many engines are more powerful than this even, with more than 470bhp in some instances.

We had expressed disbelief concerning the performance capabilities of this machine. Certainly it is very fast, we averred, but that fast? We had to go to Italy to find out for ourselves, and as we have reported, we were proven comprehensively wrong as far as maximum speed is concerned. If anything, Lamborghini's press department now appears to lean towards understatement.

What of the acceleration? These days a 0–60mph time of 5.0sec is about even par in the supercar league. We know of nothing apart from purpose-built competition cars which can match the Countach's 4.2sec. You simply give it lots of revs to break the tenacious grip of the enormous rear tyres, dump the clutch and go. It goes all the way in first gear if you ignore the red-line change-up at 58mph, and then you're up into third at 80mph, with 100mph being achieved in an almost incredible 10.0sec. Carry on and 120mph (having changed into fourth at 119mph) comes up in 14.1sec, 130mph in 17.2sec and 140 in 20.5. You can then cruise past a flat-out Jalpa before changing into top at 151mph. We passed the standing quarter-mile in 12.5sec (anything better than 14sec is extremely quick) at 113.6mph. There was not sufficient space to check out the standing kilometre, but it must take about 22 or 23sec at the most.

The figures for maximum speed and standing start acceleration are comfortably the best ever recorded by any magazine anywhere in the world for a production car. It is conceivable that they will never be bettered.

If you are a respecter of red lines on rev counters, you will never see more than 183mph if your Countach's needle works properly, for that is the road speed (ignoring tyre growth, which may be a factor) at 7,500rpm (there is a precautionary yellow sector before that, starting at 7,000rpm). One can only assume that Piero Martini's rev needle has hit the stop so often that the return spring is suffering from incipient metal fatigue. The theoretical engine speed at 195mph is about eight turns short of 8,000rpm.

The engine has an unburstable feel to it, all the way up its range, changing the note of the magnificent howl that only a highly tuned V12 can make. Shortly before maximum speed is reached the note deepens perceptibly, though it doesn't sound as if the engine is about to disintegrate. Temperatures of the water and oil both rose noticeably during our high-speed runs, but not into the danger zone.

Firing up the Countach from cold calls for a sequence of actions which almost form a ritual. Switch on the ignition and wait for the ticking of the fuel pumps to fade away. Turn the key further and you will know that the engine has started even if you are deaf, from all the opening windows and the birds flying from the trees. That ferocious, hungry growl, which you get only with multiple carburetters on a multi-cylinder engine settles into a deep rumble. It is necessary to wait a little longer for the various fluids to flow properly, particularly in the gearbox, which initially feels as if it has seized.

To withstand the loadings put through it, the gearbox for such a car needs to be very strong, and this often leads to a gearchange similar to that of a heavy goods vehicle. The siting of the Countach's box helps by obviating the need for a long linkage; the result is a very positive change and even if the movements through the slotted gate (with first offset to the left and reverse protected from accidental selection by a sprung locking tab) are rather long, it's really a question of how quickly you can move your hand. The Fichtel and Sachs clutch is very heavy (about the same as that of an Aston Vantage), and being stuck in West End traffic in a Countach late on a Friday afternoon must be an excellent exercise for building up the thigh muscles.

This is something that you simply have to put up with, but we did wonder about the unusual amount of force required of one's right foot in initially depressing the throttle. It feels as if one is on the wrong end of an over-centre situation, to coin a phrase. After that, throttle response is miraculously smooth, every tiny movement eliciting a small answer from the engine, which is what is needed in a car like this. Lamborghini's engineers are aware of this initial fierceness and are working on means to eliminate it.

Although maximum torque seems high up the range at 5,200rpm, our acceleration figures in top and fourth show that the curve must be a very flat one with, as we had decided subjectively, with plenty from 3,000rpm onwards, which means that this engine has an unusually wide useable rev band, even for a big V12. Indeed, the response to flooring the throttle at only 1,500rpm in top (about 36mph) is simply instant, smooth, turbine-like acceleration, and the figures from 40mph onwards are outstanding.

If you can afford a Countach, you'll not be worried by anything as trivial as fuel consumption, but you will want to be able to travel quite a few miles on a full tank, or rather tanks since there are two which are inter-connected. The total capacity of 26.4 gallons gives a range of over 250 miles even assuming lead-footed driving, which may result in something like 9mpg. Minimal restraint could earn up to 13mpg, and if you

take it gently (which is a fairly weird thing to do in a Countach), you might get 15 or 16mpg.

There is an advantage to be gained from taking the engine up to its rev limit on every change, but it's only a small one, and very little is lost by switching gears at 6,500rpm or so. The ratios are so well spaced that pushing the throttle to the floor in any gear at almost any speed produces the sort of acceleration that really does force your neck backwards.

If nobody told you that the brakes were servo-assisted, you'd probably not suspect it: here's another useful muscle-toning device.

The discs are all ventilated, and all mounted outboard, and they are the size of dinner plates: 11.2in at the rear and 11.8in at the front.

As with the rest of the car, it's not just what the brakes do, but the way that they do it that impresses. Repeated, punishing decelerations from extremely high speeds failed to melt the pads or boil the fluid. There was no sign of fade, no tugging from side to side, no premature locking, and barely any forward pitch, except of driver and passenger against the webbing of the seat belts. The car simply lost a great deal of speed in a very short distance. There is no option of anti-lock brakes; somehow, they would be out of character in this car.

When burbling around waiting for a gap into which to propel this projectile, one becomes aware of a few noises that are normally drowned out by the howl of the engine (even so, since much of that marvellous bellow is left behind, it is still just possible to have a conversation at over 180mph, if you can think of a good reason to do so). There is quite a lot of transmission whine in the intermediates, and the tyres and suspension make plenty of noise over surface irregularities (though no more so than is the case in a Porsche 911). However, wind noise is virtually absent, as are any creaks or rattles, which tends to confirm the belief that the chassis is impressively rigid.

In the assessment of a car's handling abilities, first impressions play an important role. There is often a single word which projects itself to the foreground of your imagination the very first time you brake, change down and turn into a bend in a car. You might drive another 1,000 miles, or 10,000, in that car, but that word will often present itself again and again. If you are alert and doing your job properly, that first impression can often encapsulate the entire feel of the car.

What is the word in this case? There isn't a direct translation of 'Countach', but that's the way it feels: spectacular, magnificent, superb, all those 'Wow!' words, certainly; somehow it just feels absolutely right. If you look at this car or the Testarossa, as you

Though entry and exit is awkward, the Countach is reasonably comfortable once you've squeezed inside it. This is a quattrovalvole.

hold the keys in your sweaty palm and prepare yourself to get in and drive it, if you consider the price and the horsepower and are easily intimidated by such considerations, you will doubtless be scared witless.

However, you then arrive at your first bend in the Countach, and its responses to your actions are so precise, and predictable, that you instantly feel that the car is working for you, whereas in some rivals you feel that you are sitting on the back of a wild animal, trying desperately to maintain the illusion of control. Driving satisfaction has no directly proportional relationship with the number of times that the machine succeeds in terrifying its driver.

The first surprise is that the unassisted steering, rack and pinion, naturally, is light in the straight ahead position even at very low speeds; then you glance at the speedometer and realise you are travelling at about 80mph. It is only when manoeuvring in a tight space that the poor lock (common to all fat-tyred supercars) and a fair degree of weight make their presence felt. Also, you can't help thinking of the cost of P7s when those front gumballs shave across the surface during a three-point (or more likely six-point) turn.

On the move, the steering writhes gently over surface irregularities, but kickback is not severe, and the tendency to follow white lines and other raised sections is never alarming. Turn into a bend, and the weight builds up. Always you can feel very easily where the front wheels are pointing, and usually only a small amount of lock is required. It is unnecessary to fight the steering.

With an overall rubber contact patch unequalled by any other road car (the rear tyres are 345/35 VR 15 on 12in rims, and the fronts are 225/50 VR 15 on 8.5in rims), it is hardly surprising that dry road grip is outstanding. But roadholding is one thing and overall handling another, and the more impressive aspects of the Countach are how well balanced it feels, how much true feel of the surface is fed to the driver via the wheel and through the chassis, and how progressively and predictably it responds to suggestions that it should change direction. Again, it is working with the driver rather than against him.

No doubt a Porsche 959, and for that matter many other four-wheel-drive cars, would leave a Countach floundering on a twisty route in poor conditions, but that would not be so in the dry. It has a lot of power to put down, and it puts it down well. The combination of more than 450 horsepower and race-car-sized tyres (even if they do have a tread pattern) demands a certain level of skill, but that admitted, there are many cars with engines of lower output which are more difficult to drive.

The point is that the Countach does not have that combination of apparently limitless grip and then abrupt breakaway which can be so fraying to the nerves, not to mention potentially damaging to the rest of the system. Instead, there is a steady feedback to the driver so that if an adjustment to the line becomes necessary, the driver can make it before a crisis is reached. Although very neutral in general terms, it does eventually push its nose wide under power in most circumstances. Ease pressure on the throttle, and it will come back on line. Presumably if you are skilled enough and the road is sufficiently wide, it is possible to balance the slide out by applying extra throttle, but that is for the ultra-confident and mega-brave.

In a tight bend, even in the dry, it is possible to punch the tail out with a brutal and sustained stamp on the throttle pedal. It isn't really necessary to indulge in such hooliganism, and the joy of the Countach is the way it can be made to flow through a series of curves, with scarcely any perceptible roll. If Active Suspension can make a car like this seem archaic, it must be truly astonishing.

Another surprising aspect of the car, and

entirely unexpected as far as we were concerned, is the comfort of the ride. Everything is relative, of course, and we are not suggesting that in this area the Countach is anything like a match for a Jaguar XJ12, but in comparison with almost any high-performance car you care to mention, the Lamborghini shines. At low speeds over rough surfaces it jiggles, but doesn't send violent shocks vertically through the spines of the occupants. Travel just a little faster and it smooths everything out quite remarkably, and at very high speed there is no tendency to float.

Development never stops, so there cannot be such a thing as the "ultimate supercar", but that is what Lamborghini and Bertone were aiming at with the Countach: a two-seater with racing car characteristics and as few compromises as possible, yet just about practical enough for it to be used on public roads rather than a race track.

Over the years, the appearance of the car has changed, but not radically: the front bumper is now colour-keyed (a process which hadn't been perfected 13 years ago), and a front bib spoiler and wheel arch extensions have been added, the former for aerodynamic considerations, the latter to envelope the much enlarged tyres, now fitted to a more modern rim design, with offset fronts and heavily inset rears. The engine cover now has a large hump at its centre to accomodate the taller Webers, and this further reduces rearward visibility via the interior mirror. Mind you, if you fit that silly rear wing, you can forget all about seeing anything of the road behind except by means of the very good door mirrors. It is remarkable how well this extraordinary shape has stood the test of time, for it still looks like the car of tomorrow.

Incidentally, the Countach was never specifically intended for the US market, but demand has been such from across the water that there is a 'Federalised' Countach with a fuel-injected engine that rather emasculates

the machine. It does have better rearward vision, for the engine cover, instead of having one large mound in its centre, has one smaller one at each side, permitting a channel of sight through its centre. To meet the '5mph' crash regulations, however, the purity of the body's line has been destroyed by front and rear bumpers whose hideousness has to be seen to be believed. Happily, although the Law is undoubtedly an ass everywhere, we haven't yet reached that level of jackassishness in Europe . . .

Underneath that extraordinary shape, with its single curve sweeping from nose to tail, underneath the beautifully hammered aluminium panels, is a 'birdcage' space-frame chassis of such complexity that it defies the imagination. For a number of different considerations, it is ideal for the engine in a mid-engined car to be located longitudinally, and that is the case in the Countach. Normally, the gearbox is then mounted behind it, in unit with the final drive. However, in the Countach, the gearbox is ahead of the engine, and the drive passes back via a shaft through the crankcase. It is a clever solution to the problem, and one which still makes sense today, even though manufacturing is made more complicated.

Attached to this frame at either end is suspension of classic racing heritage: unequal-length double wishbones, with angled coil spring/damper units and an anti-roll bar.

Getting in and out of the Countach requires a special technique. You pull the catch, and the door swings forwards and upwards to an angle of 45 degrees, aided by a hydropneumatic strut. Then you sit on the very wide sill, in the gap formed by door, roof and door jamb. It is not a big gap. After that, there are two alternative methods of gaining entry. The first is to ease your body in first, dragging your legs after you. The second is to swing the legs through under the steering wheel, trying not to entangle

The dashboard of the quattrovalvole.

The gear lever is well placed, and although the gearchange is quite heavy, it is almost impossible to select the wrong slot.

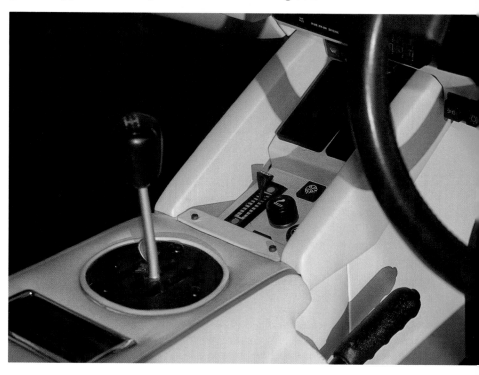

There is plenty of leather inside this quattrovalvole, *though it is not nearly as luxurious as some high-quality British cars.*

your feet in the pedals, and then to squeeze through after them. It's not too difficult once you've got the hang of it, so long as you haven't eaten too many business lunches and are reasonably fit. Evacuating the car following a rollover doesn't bear thinking about, though.

Surprisingly, the space inside the car is not too bad, and it is considerably less cramped than an Esprit, for example; nor does it give the same claustrophobic feeling. Even for tall drivers, there is just about sufficient headroom, and though it is necessary to drive with knees bent, the in/out adjustability of the steering wheel avoids dangerous contact between hands and thighs when lock is applied. The pedals are offset to the centre because of wheel arch intrusion, but they are well spaced. The handbrake lever pokes out of a recess next to the wide central console. The switches, stalks and instruments are all simple; they function well, but there is nothing in particular to mention about them. Likewise the trimming is competently executed, though it does not give that air of plush luxury that you find in an Aston Martin or the crisp, modern and efficient environment of the latest Ferraris.

The seats are of a true 'bucket' design, the frames forming a single curve from headrest to tip of cushion, and they can be adjusted for tilt as well as to slide fore and aft. They offer good lateral location and are acceptably comfortable for journeys of moderate length. A necessary detail in the passenger's footwell is a foot support bar. There are small pockets in the doors, but interior stowage space otherwise is zero. The engine cover and boot release levers are concealed in the door jamb, and the carpeted boot, though by no means large, is not too bad for this type of car. The front lid conceals a get-you-home-if-you-aren't-arrested spare tyre, the battery, the brake servo, and not much else.

On a long journey, the majority of luggage

must follow at some distance with your accountant and lawyer in the Silver Spirit.

The Countach's interior may not be claustrophobic, but the all-round view from it is not a strong point. Its forward vision is acceptable when you get used to looking through that huge pane of glass set in a shallow incline: ahead of you, it is just possible to see the highest peaks of the front wheel arches, but you must guess where the nose might be. At each side, there is a pattern of four small panes of glass. One of these can be lowered – by a manual winder – and the theory is that you can use it for paying autostrada tolls (the ones which involve a five-minute queue and a payment which often does not exceed 30p); in practice, it's necessary to open the door, unless the toll-booth operator has four-foot long arms.

Reversing a Countach in a confined space is a minor nightmare, and the preferred technique seems to be to open the door and sit on the sill, like a victorious Martin Schanche going backwards. Threading through heavy traffic, with XR3 drivers attempting to impress you with their sub-40mph car control, must be rather tiresome. This really is a car designed for the open road, and once there (with the XR3s diminishing specks in the rearview mirror, or they would be if you could see through the engine cover), visibility is not a serious hindrance.

At 150mph, the single pantograph-action wiper (with a tiny subsidiary blade floating beneath it) lifts something like an inch above the screen. This is probably a built-in safety measure, a piece of advice from the factory that you shouldn't reach that speed in the wet . . .

Until recently, Italian cars have not been known for the efficiency of their ventilation systems, which is odd for such a hot country. The Countach has air conditioning, but its performance should be considered adequate rather than outstanding. Probably in this country, where blue sky constitutes a

PERFORMANCE

Tests carried out in Italy.

Maximum speed *(mean of runs in opposite directions)* 190.1mph
Best one-way 195.2mph

Acceleration from rest:

mph	sec
0–30	1.9
0–40	2.5
0–50	3.2
0–60	4.2
0–70	5.4
0–80	6.7
0–90	8.3
0–100	10.0
0–110	11.8
0–120	14.1
0–130	17.2
0–140	20.5
Standing ¼-mile	12.5sec/113.6mph

Acceleration in single gear:

	5th	4th
40–60	6.4	6.0
50–70	6.2	4.4
60–80	5.7	3.7
70–90	5.4	3.6
80–100	5.5	3.8
90–110	5.6	4.1
100–120	5.6	4.3

Economy

Overall consumption	See text
Composite*	12.6mpg
Tank capacity	26.4 gallons
Range	333 miles

Based on government test figures (One half of 'Urban' figure, plus one quarter of each steady-speed figure (56/75mph)).

Weight

Unladen (with fuel for 50 miles) 29.4cwt

Engine

Dohc per bank (chain driven), four valves per cylinder, water-cooled 60 degrees V12 mounted ahead of rear axle line, behind gearbox, 5,167cc (bore/stroke 85.5/75mm). Seven main bearings. Compression ratio 9.5:1. Light alloy cylinder block and heads. Six Weber 44 DCNF downdraught twin-choke carburettors. Maximum power 455bhp (DIN)/7,000rpm. Maximum torque 369lb ft/5,200rpm.

Transmission

Rear-wheel drive, five-speed synchromesh gearbox, Fichtel and Sachs hydraulic dry single-plate clutch; limited-slip differential.

Internal ratios and mph/1,000rpm:

Top	0.707:1/24.4
4th	0.858:1/20.1
3rd	1.088:1/15.9
2nd	1.625:1/10.6
1st	2.232:1/7.7
Reverse:	1.960:1
Final drive ratio	4.091:1

Body/Chassis/Suspension/Steering

Tubular steel spaceframe chassis, aluminium body panels with glass fibre wheel arch inserts. Front and rear suspension, independent by unequal-length double wishbones, coil spring/damper units, anti-roll bar. Steering, unassisted rack and pinion.

Tyres/Wheels/Brakes

Pirelli P7, front 225/50 VR 15, on 8½J alloy rims, rear 345/45 VR 15 on 12J alloy rims. Brakes, ventilated discs, front 11.8in diameter, rear 11.2in diameter.

Lamborghini Countach 5000 *quattrovalvole*

Importer: Portman Lamborghini, Portman Garages Ltd, 92–108 George Street, London W1. Tel: 01–935 7633. Manufacturer: Nuova Automobili Ferruccio Lamborghini S.p.A, 40019 S.Agata Bolognese, Via Modena 12B.

Price: £54,650.00 basic plus £8,925.62 VAT plus £4,554.17 Special Car Tax, plus £300 for 'road pack' plus £100 Road Tax equals £68,529.79

COUNTACH ROAD TESTS

	LP400		LP400S	LP500S			5000QV		
	Motor, 1 November 1975	*Road & Track*, February 1976	*Road & Track*, December 1978	*Autocar*, 9 October 1982	*Car and Driver*, December 1983	*Motor*, 17 April 1984	*Autocar*, 29 May 1985	*Car and Driver*, April 1986	*Fast Lane*, September 1986
mph/sec									
0–30	2.7	3.7	2.6	2.4	2.4	2.2	2.1	2.2	1.9
0–40	3.4	4.6	–	3.3	3.1	2.9	2.7	3.0	2.5
0–50	4.4	5.5	4.6	4.4	3.8	3.6	3.5	3.8	3.2
0–60	5.6	6.8	5.9	5.6	5.4	4.8	4.9	5.1	4.2
0–70	7.5	8.2	7.7	7.0	6.6	6.0	6.0	6.1	5.4
0–80	9.0	9.6	–	8.8	8.1	7.5	7.2	7.7	6.7
0–90	11.1	–	–	10.7	10.1	9.3	9.0	9.3	8.3
0–100	13.1	13.3	14.4	12.9	12.1	11.3	10.6	11.0	10.0
0–110	15.9	–	17.7	15.3	15.0	13.8	12.3	12.9	11.8
0–120	20.3	18.2	–	18.5	18.9	17.4	15.5	16.6	14.1
0–130	–	–	–	22.4	24.5	21.5	18.5	–	17.2
0–140	–	–	–	28.0	–	27.2	21.1	–	20.5
0–150	–	–	–	37.2	–	–	25.1	–	–
0–160	–	–	–	58.0	–	–	32.1	–	–
0–170	–	–	–	–	–	–	44.7	–	–
Standing ¼	14.1	14.4	14.6	14.0	13.5	13.2	13.0	13.3	12.5
Standing km	25.2	–	–	24.9	–	24.0	23.3	–	–
5th gear									
30–50	–	–	–	9.8	8.3	–	5.8	7.6	–
40–60	–	–	–	8.2	7.7	6.6	5.8	–	6.4
50–70	12.0	–	–	7.4	–	6.3	5.8	7.3	6.2
60–80	12.6	–	–	7.1	–	6.9	5.8	–	5.7
70–90	10.3	–	–	6.8	–	7.2	5.7	–	5.4
80–100	11.0	–	–	6.8	–	7.3	5.7	–	5.5
90–110	11.4	–	–	6.5	–	7.6	5.6	–	5.6
100–120	13.7	–	–	6.8	–	8.1	5.6	–	5.6
110–130	–	–	–	7.9	–	–	5.8	–	–
120–140	–	–	–	9.7	–	–	6.7	–	–
130–150	–	–	–	14.0	–	–	8.7	–	–
140–160	–	–	–	26.4	–	–	11.3	–	–
150–170	–	–	–	–	–	–	20.7	–	–

	LP400		LP400S	LP500S			5000QV		
	Motor, 1 November 1975	*Road & Track*, February 1976	*Road & Track*, December 1978	*Autocar*, 9 October 1982	*Car and Driver*, December 1983	*Motor*, 17 April 1984	*Autocar*, 29 May 1985	*Car and Driver*, April 1986	*Fast Lane*, September 1986
4th gear									
30–50	–	–	–	6.4	–	7.0	4.5	–	–
40–60	–	–	–	5.5	–	4.7	4.5	–	6.0
50–70	–	–	–	5.2	–	5.0	4.5	–	4.4
60–80	–	–	–	5.0	–	5.0	4.4	–	3.7
70–90	–	–	–	4.9	–	4.8	4.1	–	3.6
80–100	–	–	–	4.9	–	4.8	3.8	–	3.8
90–110	–	–	–	5.0	–	5.1	4.0	–	4.1
100–120	–	–	–	5.5	–	5.9	4.3	–	4.3
110–130	–	–	–	6.8	–	–	4.8	–	–
120–140	–	–	–	8.8	–	–	5.6	–	–
130–150	–	–	–	–	–	–	7.0	–	–

heatwave, it would perform more acceptably the task of keeping occupants cool.

At times in the past, Lamborghini's standards of finish were perhaps not as high as might be wished, but now, with greater financial security, a new atmosphere of confidence in the factory, excellent working conditions, and a very well developed product, those standards have risen considerably. The Countach is as beautiful close up as it is from the other side of the street, and the panel fits are particularly impressive.

It is a crazy vision made into reality. It costs a fortune. It is totally impractical. There is no way that buying it could be justified by any rational argument, but if you are a true car enthusiast and immensely wealthy, you will feel obliged to ignore all those sensibile, puritanical, 'realistic' mumblings from one side of your brain, and listen to the other side shouting 'Countach!'

If your bank manager is unaccustomed to cheques against your account for almost £69,000, you will, like us, be considering methods of acquiring this car which do not involve the likelihood of going to prison for a few years. There never has been anything quite like it, and probably there never will be again. Perhaps the Germans make the best cars in the world, but the Italians make the most exciting, most outrageous and most marvellous one, and this is it. Countach!

6 Diablo

The Countach is history. Nobody, and nothing, can be a sex object forever – and nineteen years (since it was a far from bashful debutante) is not bad going by any standards. The Diablo is the supercar of the future – but for all its advanced technology, can it be as exciting, as desirable or as controversial, and can it last as long?

But for the Chrysler takeover, the Diablo might have been an up-dated Countach. In fact, although it has an engine of Countach derivation, it is such a different car that the change of name was not only justified, but really essential from a purist's point of view – and what other point of view can there be, for a car bearing the Lamborghini name?

As mentioned in Chapter 8, there was fierce rivalry to design the replacement for the Countach. From the beginning, Lamborghini management wished to use Marcello Gandini, who had of course been responsible for the shape of the original Countach. On the other hand, there was strong pressure from the Chrysler US design teams – as, obviously, to have designed a supercar is every automotive draughtsman's dream. But there was competition also from Italy. Giugiaro sent a 1:8-scale wooden painted model, early in the first stages of the project (1986–1987). It was apparently much along the lines of the Lotus Etna, and was rejected immediately as too bland and impersonal to be a Lamborghini. It is unknown whether Bertone presented any possible designs, but his styling house is not what it was: witness the Genesis 'people-carrier', the driver of which needs to be a person of restricted growth, compared with which even the Portofino seems elegant, modern and practical.

In the midst of the 'discussions' between Lamborghini and Chrysler about the design direction of the Diablo, the extraordinary Cizeta Moroder V16-T appeared. This was a one-off publicity stunt or else a kite-flying exercise, depending upon your point of view. Whichever the case, it concentrated the minds of those taking decisions at Lamborghini and Chrysler, and in a way that many observers would not have predicted: Chrysler took a quiet step backwards, and allowed Lamborghini management to decide who would design the Diablo and how, and Lamborghini's Italian management had an officially heated discussion (and perhaps an unofficial laugh) with Marcello Gandini, whose design was then given the go-ahead.

When questioned about the Cizeta, Gandini was relaxed and offhand: its shape was a design rejected by Lamborghini, at the time the Cizeta was being built there was no guarantee that the Diablo would be based on his design (mock-ups and clay models, he said, seemed to arrive from the USA almost every day, and every leading designer working for Chrysler US wanted his name on the next Lamborghini). A Lamborghini spokesman said in mid-1989: 'Now relations with Mr Gandini are good again, though not as perfect as before the Cizeta.'

NEW DIRECTIONS

The Countach is dead. The last of the Anniversary models was produced at Sant'Agata

Overleaf: This view emphasises the fact that the Diablo evolved from the Countach.

Above: *this view of the LP400 in 1978 shows how little the car had changed visually since its introduction compared with the Diablo* (right). *The most obvious change is that the NACA duct is now picked out in black.*

at the end of March 1990, bringing to a close a remarkable seventeen years of production. Lamborghini's replacement, the Diablo, is due to start coming down the same production line in June. I was invited to the factory to preview the new car prior to the official launch in Monte Carlo on 20 January 1990.

On paper, the Diablo looks like an updated Countach, but it is very much in tune with the times – in so far as that does not sound ridiculous when applied to a two-seater with a V12 engine putting nearly 500bhp through 335-section rear tyres.

If you thought the Gandini-designed Cizeta Moroder V16-T gave you a sneak preview of the Diablo, you were right, though magazines which promoted 'spy' shots of a test 'mule' last year as the Diablo in its final form have been proven incorrect. The front end of the Diablo – and indeed the sides of it, as far back as the rear of the doors – is very similar to the Cizeta, and it will be

hard to tell the two apart on the rare occasions that they appear in a rear-view mirror. The front wing line of the Diablo is more striking, but the side window shape (better for vision) is rather awkward, especially at its low forward extremity, where door and windscreen pillar meet front wing.

But from the 'B-posts' back, the Diablo is very much more attractive, with some excellent detailing. It is particularly pleasing from low down in the rear, its rear wings recalling the shape of the original LP500 show car, and another echo of the early Countach may be seen in the scalloped rear arches. There are a few too many apertures in the car from an aesthetic point of view, but there is a great deal of heat to be dissipated from this machine, and the Diablo looks less like a mobile food processor than some other modern mid-engined cars. Not everyone will like the new engine cover,

but it allows much better rearward vision than the tall carburettor box of the Anniversary.

Incidentally, if you really insist on impairing the rearward view, the factory has designed a new rear spoiler. Nobody at Lamborghini likes it, since (as with the Countach), it cuts down the top speed while conferring no benefit in stability. The Diablo retains the Countach's singular engine/ transmission arrangement, in which the five-speed gearbox is mounted ahead of the longitudinally-aligned 48-valve engine, and drives the rear wheels via an enclosed shaft running back through the sump. Engineering Director Luigi Marmiroli says that alternative configurations were assessed, but none was considered superior.

But the Diablo is much more than simply a reskinned Countach. The entire car has been re-engineered from bumper to bumper,

Officially introduced in January 1990, the Diablo, which replaces the Countach, is much cleaner in reality than the scoop shots of disguised prototypes suggested.

and Marmiroli (an ex-Grand Prix engineer) jokes that the only common component is the bull badge on the nose. The engine, for a start, has been enlarged from 5,169cc to 5,709cc (and is, as a consequence, slightly less 'over-square'). It produces 492bhp at 7,000rpm, and peak torque of 428lb ft is delivered at 5,200rpm; and all that is achieved with twin catalytic converters, whereas the Countach's Bosch K-jetronic injection system (for US-specification models) could not get anywhere near the carburettored version's 455bhp. The improvement, says Marmiroli, is largely due to the efficiency of Lamborghini's new sequential multi-point injection system (known as L.I.E.!) which is integrated with its electronic ignition. So now, for the first time, Lamborghini's crazy flagship will have the same engine throughout the world. The Diablo has the same gearbox worldwide too, but it is also all-new. It had to be re-designed to be attached to a transfer box for the four-wheel-drive version of the car, the Diablo VT which is due in 1991 (more of which anon). The chassis is still a multi-tubed spaceframe, but the tubes are now square in section. Though the round-section tubes are theoretically superior, Marmiroli says that the Diablo is thirty per cent stiffer than the Countach in torsion. Square tubes make production considerably easier, simplifying welds and saving weight.

Materials in the body and chassis have been carefully selected so that the most appropriate is chosen in each area. Thus, we find that high-strength alloy is used for the central passenger 'safety cell', while a lesser alloy is used for the front and rear 'crumple zones'. Much of the body continues to be panelled in aluminium (or rather aluminium alloy, which apparently improves the quality of the surface) but the front and rear sections are in composites, as are the engine cover and front lid. Lamborghini learned a great deal about the advantages and disadvantages of composites with the *Evoluzione*

Countach a couple of years ago. That was a fully composite car; it was too rigid for the barrier tests!

One of the drawbacks of the Countach was that its wheelarches did not permit the use of the 17in (432mm) rims which have been introduced in recent years and which not only give good results with the massive Pirelli P Zero tyres (F40 sizes: 245/40 at the front and 335/35 at the back), but also allow larger brake discs to be used. Actually the rears on the Diablo are the same size as before, but the fronts are now 13in (330mm) in diameter (also identical to the F40).

Anti-lock brakes (ABS) are not part of the existing or projected specification. Marmiroli says this was purely an engineering decision, not based on the difficulties of making ABS work with four-wheel drive. The intention is to leave as much feel in the hands of the driver as possible. It will be interesting to see the effects of this philosophy, which also rules out power-assisted steering – the Diablo VT will have a limited-slip front differential. Its central viscous coupling will never permit more than twenty per cent of the torque to arrive at the front wheels.

'This is not a rally car', says Marmiroli. 'Of course, with big tyres like that, you are still going to have difficulties in bad weather. Our aim with the VT, though, is to take away the traction problems which can be suffered in first gear when the driver is trying to put a lot of power on to a damp road.' The VT will also have electronically-controlled damping, but it will not have the fully 'Active' suspension or four-wheel steering favoured by some rivals whose supercars are scheduled to appear in the next couple of years. Coil springs are still preferred in Sant'Agata.

Marmiroli says he is pleased that there will be no shortage of competition for the Diablo. Two rivals are being produced by ex-Lamborghini men, Claudio Zampolli's Cizeta and the Bugatti (the latter, engineered by the great Paolo Stanzani – who created the

From the rear, the Diablo is far neater than the Anniversary Countach model.

Countach – is considered by most of those in the know to be the greater threat). The aim is to build 500 Diablos per year. That is two per day and a twenty per cent increase on the Countach's final, record-breaking year. Marmiroli believes that because the difference in cost will not be large, all Diablos will be VTs.

At under 176in (4.5m), the Diablo is the same length as a Montego, and not much longer than the Countach, the gearbox location aiding compactness. But the width has increased to more than 80in (2m), 2in (51mm) wider than the F40, and that is still barge-like even if it is 8in (203mm) narrower than the Cizeta. As well as a wider

track, the Diablo has a longer wheelbase than the Countach, which not only aids handling but improves internal space. The increased height of the car also gives better headroom, though it is still too easy to bang your head when getting in or out. The interior is considerably tidier, but remains largely conventional.

Electric operation of the windows is retained, more useful now that the windows are deeper than letterboxes, but the inappropriate provision of electric adjustment of the seats has been abandoned. The only unusual aspect of the instruments is that the two major dials are located outside the wheel rim.

Diablo details, including
'Disegno Gandini' – a clear
signal that the factory has
forgiven him for the Cizeta.

Rough castings on top of the fuel-injected V12 identify this as a pre-production engine. The injection system makes the engine substantially lower, thereby improving rearward vision.

The Countach weighed in at 29.3cwt (1,488kg) in its final form. The enlarged Diablo tips the scales at 32.5cwt (1,651kg) (the VT is almost 9.1cwt above that). This means that the power/weight ratio is marginally worsened, so the quoted acceleration figures are quite remarkable: 0–100kph in 4.09 sec, and the standing kilometre in 20.7sec, both of which are *just* better than Ferrari's staggering 21cwt (1,067kg) F40 can manage. Top speed (aided by a drag coefficient of 0.31, which is not bad for a supercar – though the frontal area is massive) is said to be 202mph (325kph), and – again, no doubt, coincidentally – that is 0.62mph (1kph) better than Ferrari's claim for the F40 . . .

Nobody (including the factory) is exactly sure how many Countaches have been made since the first production LP400 of 1974, by which time Ferruccio Lamborghini had severed all connection with the car company he had created. It is certainly less than 1,500. Volkswagen makes four times as many Golfs in a day. This leads us to the question: will the Diablo last through to the year 2006, and if so, who will then own Lamborghini?

7 Which is the World's Fastest Car?

Maximum speed is almost meaningless in the modern world, even in Germany where (at the time of writing) there remain sections of *autobahn* where there is no legal speed limit. Anyway, it's anti-social, isn't it, to go that fast? Step out of a Countach and a spotty schoolboy is bound to ask you: 'How fast does it go, mister?' Statistics show that one in every 2.7 million spotty schoolboys in the northern hemisphere grows up to be a Countach owner, so it pays to give a polite answer, just in case. This is it.

The question: 'Which is the world's fastest car?' sounds simple enough when it trips off the tongue, but it is almost impossible to answer in one sentence, let alone by merely supplying a name. It depends what you mean by 'fastest'; it also depends whether you are talking about production cars – and then how do you define a 'production car'? Presumably we are ruling out Richard Noble's Thrust 2 Land Speed Record 'car', and also racing cars, dragsters and other interesting abnormalities. But should modified 'specials' such as Ruf-Porsches and Callaway Corvettes be considered? How about limited-edition models, such as the Porsche 959 or the Ferrari F40? You see, it isn't such a simple question after all.

A 959 has been timed at just under 200mph (322kph), and an F40 at a couple of mph over that figure; a Ruf-Porsche 911 has achieved more than 210mph (338kph). But the Ruf, though it is beautifully engineered, cannot be regarded as a production car. Nor can the F40 or 959, both of which were designed and built as 'limited-edition' models.

They are like signed woodcuts by a famous artist.

We could define a production car as one which is built over a period of years, with no pre-set limit to the number that will be produced. If that is a fair definition, then there is a sound argument for the Countach as the world's fastest production car. When the last Anniversary rolled off the production line at Sant'Agata, more than 1,400 Countaches had been made, and there is – taking care with our definitions – no other car which has been produced in greater quantities of which as many have been as fast . . .

Well, that's a pretty woolly definition, and it needs some clarification: the Countach was projected from the start to do 200mph (322kph), but the original 'LP500' was a close relative to the unicorn. The LP400, though with a few more holes in it than in Gandini's original design (in order to stop the water from boiling), was nevertheless very clean aerodynamically, and it was capable of almost 186mph (300kph). That was back in 1974, and in that period there was nothing on the road that could get near it. Perhaps the closest was the Daytona, the fastest production Ferrari for quite a few years, which was perhaps 10mph (16kph) short of the Countach's speed.

The LP400S, with its fatter tyres and widened arches significantly increasing the frontal area, was at least 15.5mph (25kph) slower than its predecessor – and that is before we discuss the gigantic rear wing. Without the wing, then, the speed would have been perhaps 170mph (273.5kph), and burdened with it, something under 160mph (257kph) could be expected.

An opinion – or perhaps a myth – has been expressed that the Countach, without this wing, was unstable. I can report, having sat in a 5000 *quattrovalvole* with around 8,000rpm on the rev counter in fifth gear (we'll consider, shortly, just how fast that was), that the car ran absolutely arrow-straight. Apparently, this stability was achieved by careful tuning of the ride height and attitude (the car was tilted forwards at an angle imperceptible to the naked eye) because early QVs did apparently suffer from worrying frontal lift. I cannot give a personal opinion on the stability of the LP500S or the LP400S, never having been in either.

TESTING TIMES

So how fast is the fastest Countach model, the 5000 *quattrovalvole* (the Anniversary is mechanically identical, but its aerodynamics may make a significant difference to its top speed, in either direction)? The car in which I timed the top speed was, I believe, a normal factory model. It was the property of Pierluigi Martini, the Grand Prix driver, and he had been invited by the factory to demonstrate to me the maximum speed of his Countach, because they were worried about the insurance position if a journalist wrote himself off at the wheel of one of their cars. Why this should be improved with the journalist in the passenger seat, I do not know, but as is well known, Grand Prix drivers never crash . . .

Sant'Agata lies several hundred miles north of Nardo, the fastest test track in Europe, and there is no other suitable testing location nearby – apart from the *autostrada*, where of course it is totally illegal to attempt to do such things, even when the interesting Italian custom of putting 'Prova'

plates on the car is employed. This means 'Testing', and stands in the No Man's Land between trade plates and *carte blanche*. (It would certainly be easier to talk your way out of a speeding offence in a Lamborghini in northern Italy than in, for example, an Aston Martin Vantage on the A5 near Newport Pagnell, unless you happen to be a member of the Royal Family.)

Having been trained quite a few years ago on the now defunct *Motor* magazine, I have always done my testing as professionally as conditions will allow. I can vouch 100 per cent for the acceleration figures we recorded for the *quattrovalvole*, but the top speed requires a note of explanation.

The acceleration figures were achieved with a Peiseler fifth wheel and properly calibrated electronic recorder. I asked Lamborghini tester Valentino Balboni to do the tests for me, and he responded with relish. He knows the Countach so well that on the windless day of the test, conducted in opposite directions on the public road between two villages to the north of the factory, there was barely a variation from one run to the next. It would have taken me at least four runs to discover the best technique for getting this car off the line crisply, but even then I suspect I'd have had difficulty quite matching Valentino's take-off – with just a chirp of tyres and minimal wheelspin – and impressively flicked gearchanges.

You can read the full list of times in the *Fast Lane* road test reproduced in Chapter 4 but the key figures are 0–60mph (0–96.5kph) in 4.2sec, 0–100mph (0–161kph) in 10.0sec, and 0–140mph (0–225kph) in 20.5sec, with the standing quarter-mile in 12.5sec.

It is interesting to compare these figures with those published in *Autocar* the previous year (*see* Chapter 4).The differences may be due to development in the car over the period, or else perhaps to variations in the tolerances of the two engines. *Autocar's* engine was apparently almost brand new,

The quattrovalvole *without side skirts.*

and therefore should have been tighter, which is reflected in marginally worse outright acceleration. The single-gear figures in *Autocar* are also a bit slower, but within the range that can be produced by different ambient conditions, except below 60mph (96.5kph). It seems that the engine of *Autocar's* test car picked up more cleanly below 3,000rpm.

The Porsche 959 is fractionally quicker (to 60mph (96.5kph) in 4.2sec, 100 (161) in 9.7 and 140 (225) in 19.2) but not enough to be noticeable on the road. The Ferrari F40, given lots of throttle and a brutal attitude to the clutch, will scream to 60mph (96.5kph) from rest in 3.9sec, to 100 (161) in 7.8, and will pass the 140 (225) mark in 14.0sec (all figures recorded by *Fast Lane* magazine). But is an F40 a road car?

There are several ways of recording maximum speed. The most efficient, though only if it is meticulously set up (which is not always the case), is with the use of either light beams or radar, by which in the latter case I do not mean a hand-held radar gun as used by some police forces; using one of those, I once recorded my desk, on the fifth floor of an office block in Sutton, travelling at 27mph. But if we want scrupulous accuracy, a radar system is fully dependable only if the speed of a car is measured over a distance, such as one kilometre. To do that, you need the controlled conditions of a test track.

It is possible to record maximum speed with a 'fifth wheel' but at speeds of well over 150mph (241kph), apart from the fact that the drag of the equipment will reduce the car's speed capability to an unpredictable degree, it would be irresponsible to attempt such a stunt on the public highway. The image of an apparently well-attached fifth wheel becoming free of a test car and launching itself into orbit at MIRA will stay with me forever (the equipment was never found, having disappeared into a deep gully covered in dense undergrowth). The consequences of that kind of thing on a public road could be messy.

On this occasion, at Lamborghini, there were no simple alternatives to the rather primitive method of taking a set of digital stopwatches and recording the time taken between kilometre posts on the *autostrada*. So that's what we did. Finding a gap in the traffic when you're hacking along at that speed is difficult, and it took us all morning and part of the afternoon.

At 160mph (257kph) even a wide three-lane highway with a hard shoulder seems to open ahead of you like a zip. I had experienced this many times in various cars. Go faster and the effect is extraordinarily exaggerated. Tiny specks on the horizon increase in size and accelerate with remarkable rapidity into recognisable shapes.

You have to be fully alert and must make correct decisions while there is still time to do so. Travelling at more than 180mph (290kph), even in as good a car as a Countach, is quite different from doing 120mph (193kph) in a Golf GTi or even 150mph (241kph) in a Porsche 944 Turbo, simply because you are covering one mile every twenty seconds, and 264 feet every second. There is no room for error.

We recorded a flying kilometre time in one direction of 11.46sec, which gives a speed of 195.2mph (314.1kph). The speedometer was indicating 199mph (320kph). In the opposite direction, a few minutes later, we went between the posts in 12.1 sec, which is 184.9mph (297kph). This provides a mean of opposite directions of 190.1mph (305.8kph).

Some doubt has, I understand, been expressed about these figures, though never directly to me. I can only state that I conducted the tests as diligently and honestly as possible, and I have considered all the possible areas in which inaccuracy could creep in. I have had a great deal of experience in timing cars with stopwatches, and reckon I'm as accurate as anyone. Let us suppose, however, for the sake of argument,

The quattrovalvole *with side skirts.*

Ferrari's F40 weighs 21.5cwt and produces almost 480bhp. It is staggeringly fast, but its spartan interior and poor finish make the Countach (right) seem, by comparison, a practical every-day car. This F40 is in the collection of Nick Mason, Pink Floyd drummer and gentleman racer.

that I consistently under-timed the car through the kilometre posts by 0.2sec. That then gives us an average of the two directions of 186.8mph (300.5kph). Let us further suppose that the kilometre posts in question were one per cent (that's ten metres, or eleven yards) closer together than they should have been. Now it's odd that I should have chosen – at random – two pairs which were each ten metres short of a kilometre apart, but no matter. That still gives a top speed of 185mph (298kph), and leaves the Countach on the top of the tree – if we're talking about production cars.

Living with a Countach

Given that it's necessary for anyone who contemplates the purchase of a Countach (or any Lamborghini) not only to be immensely wealthy but also fairly insane, it seems strange that Lamborghini bothers to include so much detail in the handbook, which for the standard-issue version given with the Anniversary is printed in three languages (French and English as well as Italian). The English is of a remarkably high standard.

There are sections not only on how to jack the car up to change a wheel, how to change the oil, and on the regularity of servicing, but also on adjusting the carburettors, checking the ignition timing, bleeding the brakes, and even on washing the car.

Mind you, since owning a Lamborghini qualifies as a hobby, it is far more likely that a Countach owner will perform one or more of these chores than his wealthy neighbour who runs a Porsche 959 or a Testarossa.

The Countach's V12 should be fairly well run-in before the car is delivered – each one is operated on the test-bed for several hours before installation in 'a vast cycle of trials'. However, running-in procedures are still recommended. Until 1,500 miles (2,500km), it is suggested that 4,000rpm should not be exceeded, rising to 5,000rpm until a total of 3,000 miles (5,000km) is passed, and then 6,000rpm until 4,350 miles (7,000km).

They want you to take this seriously. The handbook's warning is as follows: 'It is important to move from one running-in stage to the next with great care and caution: never accelerate flat-out, run the vehicle at its maximum permissible speed for no more than a few seconds at a time, and carry out regular checks on **oil pressure** and **oil and water temperatures**. For the first 1,000km, avoid **braking** sharply or for long periods.'

At least as important is the advice given elsewhere in the handbook to drive the car gently until all its fluids have warmed up thoroughly. The suggested 12 miles (20km) may be exaggerated, but it does show that this is not an 'ordinary' car. It deserves to be treated with a measure of respect.

At its first service, after 1,000 miles or 1,500km, the Countach will have a change of oil and oil filter, and your friendly local technician in his immaculate white coat will also make a thorough check of the fuel and cooling systems. Oil levels for the clutch, gearbox and differential should be checked, and the brake pads, hydraulic system and handbrake inspected. The tension of all belts should be checked.

Then, at 2,250 miles (3500km), it's new oil plus filter again, the heads are tightened and there are checks on valve clearance, chain tension, spark plugs, carburettor tuning, air filters and water pump. Repeat checks are carried out on most of the equipment previously examined, plus a few more.

Thereafter, Lamborghini recommends a major service at 5,000 miles (7,500km), another at 10,000 (15,000km), and every 10,000 miles thereafter. That's rather higher than one might expect, and is probably a response to the fashion of longer service intervals in more normal, everyday cars (like Porsches). The diligent Lamborghini owner, like his Aston-owning friends, will probably wish to have the car checked every 5,000 miles (7,500km) at most, but of course a great deal depends on the type of use to which the car is put.

The rev counter readings on the runs in question made sense in relation to the car's gearing in comparison with slower runs earlier (when even Martini had considered it prudent to back off for traffic). The red sector of the rev counter starts at 7,500rpm – there's a precautionary yellow sector marked 500rpm lower down the scale, which translates into 183mph (294kph). Martini's rev needle was hovering around the 8,000rpm mark on our fastest run. I am personally fully satisfied that the car achieved a mean speed of 190mph (306kph).

The Italian Ministry of Transportation timed the 5000 *quattrovalvole* at 292.2kph or 181.6mph at Nardo. The car reached that speed from rest in only 62sec, a feat that could perhaps be equalled by the 959, but beaten among road cars only by the F40 – which can reach 170mph (273.5kph) in 25sec. It must be borne in mind that at the speeds we are considering here, tyre scrub certainly removes a few mph, even on a gently-banked circuit such as Nardo.

Actually, it doesn't make a lot of difference to me. I do not regard the Aston Martin Zagato as a lesser machine because it is probably a few mph slower than the Countach. I do not sneer at the Testarossa because it is undoubtedly slower. But if anyone does care, and the question is asked about which is the world's fastest production car, I always say that it's the Countach, and that it does 190mph. I know – I was there. 'But', I will then add, 'your question is not as simple as it seems . . .'

8 The Rivals

Are they really rivals? Or are they alternatives? The Countach is such an individualistic car that in truth there is only one car with which it can be compared – and that car is entirely different. Life is full of paradoxes.

To many people, especially those who have driven neither car, it may seem logical to suggest that the Countach's closest 'rival' is the Ferrari Testarossa. It simply is not so, for reasons to which I shall return. In my view, and paradoxical as it may seem, the Aston Martin Vantage is the only car in the world which can be put in the same category as the Lamborghini Countach.

The two cars are so different in many ways, one is so traditionally English that

Aston Martin's Vantage, so different in many ways from the Countach, is nevertheless more comparable to it than any other car in the world, and the two companies also have a great deal in common. This is a 1984 version, fitted with unsuitable Pirelli P7s.

Constructed in the 1960s, Lamborghini's main factory building is where LM002s and Diablos are made and was previously where the Countach was created. Ventilation and light inside are the equal of any other factory in the motor industry.

the traditions it embodies no longer exist except in the imagination; the other is the essence of all things Italian. It is impossible to imagine an Aston Vantage being made in Bologna, or a Countach in Newport Pagnell. It is this integrity, this pride of engineers, designers and craftsmen, which the two cars share, and their different natures are merely the expression of this.

Aston Martin's factory, sprawling untidily across both sides of a busy road and featuring, with superb irony, a cottage as what could amusingly be described as 'corporate headquarters' is entirely unlike the Brave New World architecture of the Sant'Agata factory. Yet if you step inside each, you will find craftsmen carrying out the same types of task. Andrew Nahum wrote in *Fast Lane* in May 1984 after a visit to Sant'Agata:

'The shop floor presents an astonishing sight. Where else, under one roof, can the eye range from a machinist turning a crankshaft to trimmers fitting out a personalised edition with soft ivory hides? One might almost call it a scene from another age, evoking echoes, perhaps, of the Lagonda factory at Staines around 1948, though that would not be quite fair, because the products themselves are so exceptional.

'The machine tools are generally elderly – no turret and few capstan lathes for example. Machinists making components like cranks and camshafts with comparatively high repetition rates do so without the benefit of quick-change tool posts.

'Cutting tools, drills, reamers and taps are all changed the old-fashioned way with chuck key or spanner. There are few gauges

Countach production line at the Lamborghini factory.

either, or machine tools with digital dimensional readouts – hand-held micrometers check progress on turning big end journals after each cut. All in all, the work is on a level with a small jobbing precision engineer or prototype shop – and with older equipment than many.

'None of this implies, though, that standards of accuracy are compromised – they can be maintained without expensive automatic machinery, when the human skills are there, and when personal commitment to quality throughout the factory is so high.

'Some jobs on site are surprising, though. It would hardly seem worthwhile for Lamborghini to make fairly trivial components like exhaust manifold flanges in house, but make them they do, flame-cutting the blanks, and trueing them up with fairly laborious hand-grinding. To be fair, one should perhaps note that when opened, the factory was well equipped by the standards of its day. It's just that, since then, many troubled years have slipped by without new investment, and have left it perhaps 12 years behind in production facilities. In fact, the only high-tech equipment consists of three '70s vintage Olivetti numerically-controlled machining centres, used for complex jobs like machining the crankcases and cylinder heads for the V8 and V12 engines. These are a heritage of Ferruccio Lamborghini's attempt to build 2,000 Urracos – smaller, "more affordable" Lamborghinis that would aim for the Porsche and Ferrari Dino market slot.

'Along the rest of the lines, fitters weigh and match pistons individually, grind and blend inlet manifolds to ports, measure, assemble and check by hand, exactly like a specialist racing shop.'

Much of the investment which to that point had been lacking has since been made at Sant'Agata, but that gives a powerful flavour of the way things were for much of the Countach's existence. The main differences between that and the Newport Pagnell factory are that the English company was invested in earlier, and that not everything is under one roof. There are *several* ramshackle old sheds, which look as if they were designed for the production of Sopwith Camels, never mind Spitfires! Also, a significant section of the Aston factory is taken up by the wood shop. For a reason which no one has yet explained, British car manufacturers (Rolls-Royce, Aston Martin and Jaguar in particular) have a unique advantage over the rest of the world in the way they design, make and install veneered-wood finishes. Mercedes-Benz's wood looks more like plastic, BMW's as if a skilled amateur had polished a length of two-by-four from a do-it-yourself store. Some Italian manufacturers, particularly De Tomaso's Maserati, have in recent years attempted to use wood inside their cars, with predictably tasteless, ludicrous results. Lamborghini has not done so, and if it does, it will be on Detroit's orders.

The interior of a Lamborghini does contain leather, and wool carpeting (neither done as well as in Newport Pagnell, Crewe or at Browns Lane), and what they should aim for is a compromise between comfort and function. But you do not have to look hard to see the similarities between the two companies, especially in machining, panelbeating, engine assembly, painting and testing.

Also, neither company – unlike Ferrari – does its own casting. The enormous investment involved in a foundry is beyond their means, and in the case of Lamborghini, located close to Bologna and Modena, the wonder is that so much is done in-house: the former town in particular is the Florence of the car industry. There are roundabouts whose every exit is covered in signs to machine shops, welders, coachbuilders, chassis specialists, panel beaters, engine builders and repairers, electrical shops, transmission specialists, paint shops and trimmers. I do not believe that there is any town in the world with such a wide range of engineering craft skills.

It is interesting to note, also, that both Aston Martin and Lamborghini have had chequered histories, though Aston Martin's stretches back many more years. Both of them clung on to their existence by their fingertips through the 1970s, and their final absorption into large American corporations occurred within months of one another. By contrast, the Ferrari Testarossa, although a marvellous achievement in its own way, feels like a manufactured object rather than something produced by craftsmen. Some Lamborghini enthusiasts dismiss the Testarossa as 'a very nice Fiat', which is rather unfair; let's hope that the Diablo does not become a 'very nice Chrysler', which would be even worse.

It cannot be denied, though, that the Testarossa is rather softly sprung, with impressive ride quality for this type of car. It is also relatively soft in its damping, and this – combined with a rather high centre of gravity thanks to the engine being installed above the gearbox – makes it rather a handful when you're pushing it hard. It is a much more suitable product if you plan to go to a West End nightclub. Apart from looking very impressive, all twelve cylinders fire up first time, every time, on the key, its all-round visibility is not too bad, and it isn't difficult or tiring to drive if you don't push it near its high limits.

But if you want a car to take by the scruff of the neck and have a really good time in,

The door frames are individually fitted to each car, but then removed to facilitate assembly of other components. This shot clearly shows the composites used in the floorpan.

Assembling a car as complex as the Countach is a long and labour-intensive process. It is fascinating to watch the beast in various stages of completion on the production line.

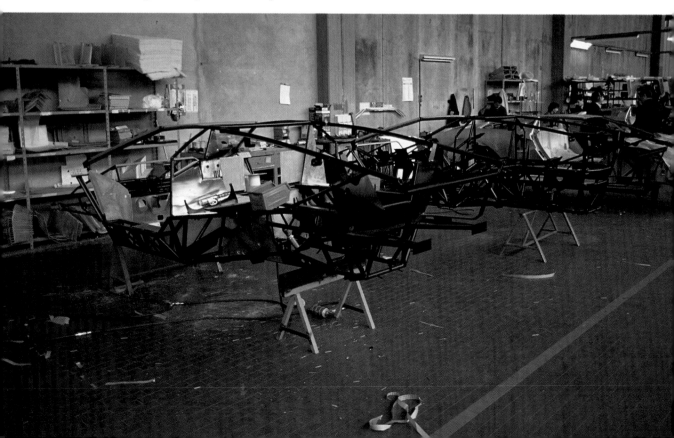

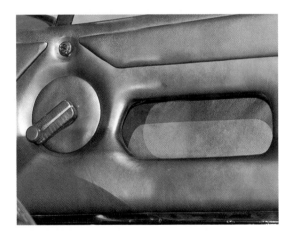

LP5000S interior shots, proving that blue and black do not mix well.

and you have sufficient skill to keep it pointed in the right direction, then the Testarossa is simply not in the same league as the Countach.

'THE LAST REPRESENTATIVES OF A VANISHING BREED...'

The Countach is a beautiful object with an almost animal nature. Along with the Aston Martin Vantage, they are the last representatives of a vanishing breed. Their replacements will not be slower in a straight line, and they will certainly be easier to drive quickly. They will be easier to get into and start, lighter to drive in traffic, easier to see out of, perhaps more manufactured than crafted. They will be rather more practical and 'user-friendly'.

But some of the individuality – and with it some of the thrill – will have gone. That is not a criticism of Ford or Chrysler – Aston Martin and Lamborghini would in any event have been forced into the directions they have gone (indeed they had already begun to move towards fuel-injected engines before the takeovers). It is merely an observation that the world moves on, and it is impossible to rationalise why one should in some ways prefer an engine which is a pig to start whether hot or cold (different techniques being required in each circumstance), which takes a long time to warm up and settle down once coaxed into life, and which is attached to a gearbox which refuses to permit the use of second gear until its oil has warmed up.

I suspect that it will only be those who have driven a Countach or a Vantage (or one or two cars from earlier years) who will understand the feelings I have about this.

Incidentally, and not that this is relevant to the point in hand, I cannot imagine seeing a sign at Porsche similar to the one above a machinist's work station at Rolls-Royce's Crewe factory, beautifully hand-written in Gothic script: 'The floggings will continue until morale improves', but I can imagine seeing that at Aston Martin and, I think, at Lamborghini. The Italians take their pleasures very seriously, but they also have a robust sense of humour, and the artisans of Lamborghini understand fully the deliciously paradoxical absurdity of their work.

How about the rest of the competition?

It seems likely that the Cizeta Moroder V16-T will remain only as an interesting historical footnote.

Maserati hasn't made a car worth considering – in this or any other context – since the Bora and Merak were discontinued. But once Alejandro de Tomaso has been eased out, new management installed and new investment available, what an opportunity for somebody that would be to revive a great name of the past. (Curiously, the De Tomaso Pantera, one of the great survivors, is actually a terrific car in its own way, if you aren't too tall. It's like a less expensive Countach without the refinement or the pedigree.)

Lotus has never built a car to rival the Countach, though its charge-cooled Esprit Turbo SE is a sort of poor man's version (well, not *that* poor). However, the forthcoming supercar, with a V8 or V12 engine, four-wheel drive, four-wheel steering, 'Active' damping control, and all manner of other modern technical devices, might be a direct competitor to the Diablo.

The Japanese manufacturers are already showing signs of stepping aggressively into territory hitherto dominated by BMW and Mercedes-Benz (the fact that Jaguar is more 'specialised' and rather quirky in its funny old British way makes it less vulnerable). This year it's the 730/735 and the ageing lesser S-class models which are under threat; next time it could be the 750i and the 560. Tokyo is on the war-path, and the Japanese are not renowned for their mercy.

The Porsche 959 is not a production car. Can it therefore be compared with the Countach?

It seems entirely inconceivable that companies like Lamborghini and Aston Martin could ever be harmed by Japanese competition, unless Chrysler and Ford devalued the marques to the extent that they were indistinguishable from the Japanese approach of vigorous marketing, flashy styling and access to a universal parts bin (as well as, let's be fair, some exceptionally good engineering).

It is hard to guess at this stage how the Bugatti will fit into this picture – will it be a high-tech rival to the Diablo and Lotus, or will it instead be the true spiritual successor to the Countach? We shall have to wait and see.

One of the world's greatest sports cars currently is American. Indeed, it could be argued that the Chevrolet Corvette ZR-1 is the world's greatest all-round sports car. It costs a lot less than the others with which it must compete, but it has a terrific specification, even if its Lotus-developed 32-valve V8 engine doesn't quite have the claimed 380bhp and cannot quite manage the suggested 180mph (290kph). It is a superbly engineered car. But once again, it is likely to attract a different buyer from the Countach customer (although he might well buy both!).

That other alleged American supercar, the Vector (created by Jerry Weigert), has yet to prove itself. Weigert has talked of 235mph (378kph) from a 1,000bhp engine, and has said that there is a production line going. He has dismissed Porsche, Ferrari and Lamborghini as: 'Some junk from Italy or Germany' . . .

Ferrari's F40 is a magnificent achievement from a technical point of view, but it isn't a production car in the same sense as the Countach, and really, it can only just be classified as a road car. It isn't quite a racing car either, so it's rather hard to decide exactly what it is, apart from a beautifully engineered investment.

Someone who buys a Porsche will be unlikely to buy it instead of a Countach. If we're into national stereotypes, there could not be clearer examples of 'Italian flair' and

Porsche's 959 lacks the charisma of the Italian supercars. It is interesting that Porsche lost money building it, while Ferrari made huge profits from the simpler and quicker F40.

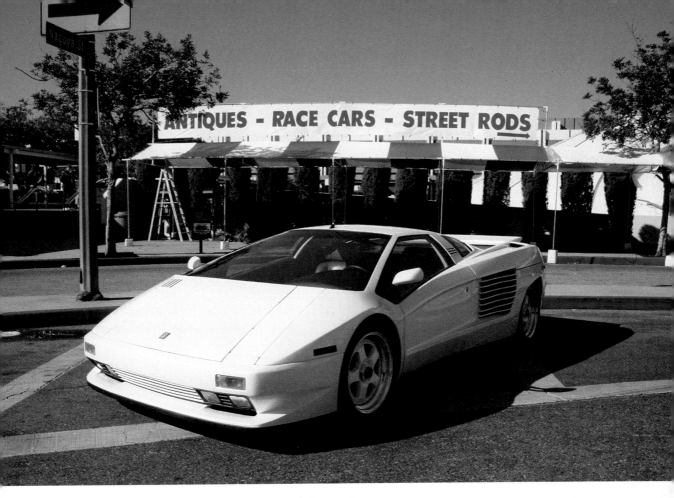

The Cizeta Moroder, with its transversely-mounted V16 engine, was one of the more extraordinary creations of Northern Italy in the late 1980s. Engineered by former Lamborghini man Claudio Zampolli, and in a body by Gandini, it made its debut at the 1989 Los Angeles Auto Show. Production run so far has been one. Today it looks like a Diablo wearing disguise panels.

'German efficiency' than Lamborghini and Porsche. Porsche's cars are very good indeed, especially the 911 Carrera Club Sport which – of all the cars recently built by Porsche – is the true enthusiast's choice (rather than the 911 Turbo, even). But they are, by comparison, everyday cars. Indeed, they are designed to be used as such, and the production methods in Stuttgart are very different, impressive and modern and with minimum wastage of time or materials.

Like the F40, the 959 is not a production car, but it is at least a fully practical road car; indeed, that scarcely does it justice – it's the most technically-advanced and efficient road car yet produced by any manufacturer in the world . . . Is that what we want from a supercar?

9 Lamborghini as a Company

The Lamborghini car company began as a surprising offshoot of a tractor manufacturer. It might seem more logical that it is now part of a worldwide car corporation. But it was an *Italian* tractor manufacturer . . .

Any company, even if it begins as the imaginative vision of one man, soon takes on a momentum of its own, and it is not uncommon for companies to collapse, or fade away slowly, when their founders die, lose interest or move out for other reasons.

Against all the odds, Lamborghini continues to exist today, and up to the point of writing at least, it remains unquestionably (and despite extensive changes in management since his departure) the child of one man: Ferruccio Lamborghini. He never lost interest, but (quite reasonably, it seems to me) he decided, after a long and unequal struggle, that there was no reason why his favourite company, indeed his obsession, should bankrupt him completely. It remains to be seen whether Chrysler fully appreciates and understands the child it has adopted, though the signs are (at least superficially) more encouraging than they were a couple of years ago.

In a sense, the Countach was the last real Lamborghini. Ferruccio had run the factory up to 1971 like a benevolent dictator. His was the vision, and he employed the best people to turn that vision into reality: Stanzani, Bizzarrini, Dallara, Bertone, Gandini, Bob Wallace and many others. It was his company, and they were his cars, and he was justifiably proud of it all. But 1971 marked a turning point in his financial affairs. From then on he could not devote as much time as he wanted to the car factory, even though it was his consuming passion.

Italy went through a dangerous period of trade union problems in the early 1970s, which made Britain's difficulties seem mild by comparison, at least in terms of the air of violence. The country was on the very brink of civil war. Alfa Romeo's bosses had to operate from a clandestine office in the centre of Milan, travelling to and from it in bullet-proofed cars: they dared not enter their own factory for fear of assassination.

Amid all the industrial unrest, there was an agricultural crisis in Italy, and this naturally had a dire effect on the tractor company which Lamborghini had founded after World War II, and which had enabled him to become a car manufacturer at a time when the ceiling on profits was not visible.

In 1972, with Countach development in full progress, a large order from Bolivia for agricultural equipment was cancelled. The effect was immediate and severe. Lamborghini had to cut his losses. He began to sell off his companies, and was forced to sell fifty-one per cent of his share in Lamborghini Automobili to Georges-Henri Rossetti, a Swiss businessman. Ferruccio eventually retired to his estate at Casteglione del Lago, to produce wines bearing his name.

At this point, the factory was at its most vulnerable. Production of the ill-fated Urraco was not yet underway, the Miura was overshadowed by the company's new star, and the Jarama was not a great sales success. Only the Espada kept the turnover relatively healthy. The decision to build the Countach as a limited-production car was taken in May 1972, and that was virtually the last action taken by Ferruccio Lamborghini in the company which still bears his name.

His foresight in taking that decision should never be under-estimated, though it may have seemed at the time (perhaps even to him) like a last defiant gesture. He was the first to see the full potential of a limited-series of truly high-performance cars in generating income and publicity: he paved the way for Ferrari's GT0 and F40, Porsche's 959, and Aston Martin's Zagato coupe and Volante. Also, that decision to build the Countach was largely instrumental in steering the company through still more difficult financial waters in later years. Without such a product, the company would either have disappeared without trace or possibly ended up within Alejandro de Tomaso's little empire; some would say there is not much to choose between those two eventualities.

During 1973, Ferruccio became increasingly remote, while Rossetti's visits to the factory were rare. This was a vital period in the development of the Countach, and by one of life's crueller ironies it coincided with a worldwide oil-crisis. It later turned out that the world was not actually running out of oil, and that the problem was more the result of an international power struggle, but as with all psychosomatic ailments, they are real enough to the sufferer.

In Britain, a temporary overall speed limit of 50mph (80kph) was imposed, the kind of measure which governments introduce to demonstrate that they are 'Taking Action'. The price of petrol shot up and petrol coupons were printed, though never issued. Similar measures were introduced, or at least discussed, in many other countries.

The major car manufacturers switched their engineering and marketing resources to smaller, more economical models, and it was predicted by some pundits that within a few years (as soon as existing models were phased out), no one would have an engine with a capacity exceeding three litres; some even suggested that two litres would be the upper limit.

This was hardly the ideal time to launch a to-hell-with-you car like the Countach, when even the most wealthy were unwilling to be identified as conspicuous consumers of an allegedly dwindling resource.

Somehow, Lamborghini managed to struggle through the 1970s. There were some good engineers there, but the company was under-financed and feebly managed. During this period, remarkably, the factory won the contract to develop a supercar for BMW. It has been suggested that much of BMW's development money was diverted into the Cheetah project (forerunner of the LM off-road vehicle). At one stage, the Germans could have bought Lamborghini for virtually nothing, but they were unwilling to invest any further in Italy. Instead they took over the supercar project themselves, turned it into the M1 (which was designed and built by Giugiaro), and lost even more money.

Despite numerous revisions and intensive development work, the Urraco was never as successful as it needed to be, and as it, the Espada and Jarama faded out, gradually Lamborghini meant Countach and vice versa.

In 1977 and 1978, with orders flowing in and no serious technical problems, Lamborghini was nevertheless on the verge of financial collapse, due to inept management. Stanzani and Bob Wallace had left in 1975, and although Dàllara was around, once more it was only on an occasional freelance basis.

Demand for the Countach at this time was high, but ironically only sixteen were produced in 1978, because of cash-flow crises. There wasn't enough money to pay for assembly components, and there wasn't always enough to pay the wage bill. Production of the Countach and Silhouette was

Lamborghini's rampant bull symbol is also the trademark for some of the world's finest engineering.

even halted for some time, because – as unbelievable as it may seem – of a shortage of components. There was also an expensive lawsuit with the American company MTI over an abortive attempt to build an off-road vehicle.

Georges-Henri Rossetti and his partner René Leimer, who presided over this unholy mess, finally gave up, and Judge Mirone in August 1978 entrusted the running of the company to an intelligent accountant, Alessandro Artese, who worked desperately hard with a small group of enthusiasts (among them Ubaldo Sgarzi, as effective a sales manager as a company like Lamborghini could wish for).

In this period, Giulio Alfieri, who had been dismissed by Alejandro de Tomaso after twenty-five years working for Maserati (including the period when the trident emblem was attached to real sports cars), joined as engineering director. Alfieri saw Lamborghini through some tough times, but his engineering approach was really out of date at a time when high technology was required in order to meet ever-increasing legislation.

Things often get worse before they get better, and 1979 was a tough year in which the factory produced only forty-four of the Countach LP400S. At the end of 1979, Hubert Hahne, Klaus Steinmetz and Raymond Neumann put together a rescue package, but they were unable to fulfil the guarantees requested, and on 28 February 1980, Lamborghini was declared bankrupt and put into receivership.

As so often in Lamborghini's history, wealthy enthusiasts came to the rescue. On this occasion, one could describe the action as enlightened investment. The two guardian angels came in the shape of Romano Bernadoni, Director of Emilianauto in Bologna, and Achilli Motors of Milan, the world's leading Lamborghini dealers. By financing components for the cars they needed, they kept the factory ticking over. But at best this could only be a short-term solution: the factory needed effective management.

THE MIMRANS

Early in 1980, the next rescuer of the company appeared in the perhaps unlikely form of Patrick Mimran, the twenty-four year old heir to a large French commercial business, and his older brother Jean-Claude. Young Patrick Mimran took over the management of the company in July. It was renamed 'Nuova Automobili Ferruccio Lamborghini S.p.A.'.

He was not only a Lamborghini enthusiast, but he also understood business principles and had the ability to select people of the right calibre to whom he could delegate responsibility. He was exactly what Lamborghini needed.

By the end of 1980, the factory had produced eighty-eight of the LP400S, admittedly still a trickle rather than a flow of cars, but nevertheless a major improvement. Mimran was Chairman, with his associate Emile Novaro as Administrator, Alfieri as General Manager and Sgarzi as Sales Manager. Confidence in the future of the company gradually returned, for the first time since Ferruccio's departure.

On 3 May 1981, the courts in Bologna had decided on the sale of the factory, and Mimran bought it, lock, stock and barrel, for 3,850,000,000 lire (approximately £1,670,000).

For the next six years, he worked hard to set Lamborghini back on course. He allowed it to survive when it could easily have collapsed. Confounding those who thought him too young and inexperienced for such a daunting task, he proved a shrewd manager and an expert at selecting the most appropriate people to key jobs.

He put the pride back into Sant'Agata. Without someone like him, even if Lamborghini had survived it would have been in no position to refuse to have terms dictated to it by an empire-building corporation such as Chrysler.

MIMRAN SELLS OUT TO CHRYSLER

In 1987, Patrick Mimran sold his share in Lamborghini to the Chrysler Corporation of the USA. Chrysler's Italian-American boss, Lee Iacocca, had been interested for some time in acquiring an Italian supercar manufacturer. He had bought fifteen per cent of Maserati from Alejandro de Tomaso a couple of years previously.

However, as Iacocca should have known from his years at Ford, de Tomaso is not the easiest man with whom to do business. Had Lamborghini not become available at what Chrysler clearly regarded as a fair price – reportedly $30 million – it is quite likely that Maserati would have been completely

---

Giulio Alfieri

The guiding light behind Maserati – for twenty-five years from 1953 – when that company was producing some great cars, Alfieri was one of the leading engineers of the post-World War II period. He was dismissed by Alejandro de Tomaso not long after the latter acquired Maserati from Citröen. In 1978, Alfieri was brought to Lamborghini as an engineering consultant by the accountant Alessandro Artese, and when the Mimrans arrived in Sant'Agata, he was appointed Chief Engineer and Plant Manager.

He had overall control of Lamborghini Engineering from 1978 until the mid-1980s, and was responsible for the Jalpa, and for developing the LP400S into the LP500S, and finally the 5000 *quattrovalvole*.

However, there is some doubt that he actually designed the *quattrovalvole* engine. He created an intermediate car (not to be confused with the *Evoluzione*), still with carburettors, which was intended to bridge the gap between Countach and Diablo. But only one, technically interesting but ugly prototype was built (which still exists), and it was a blind alley which wasted valuable development time.

taken over by Chrysler, and entirely changed. In Maserati's case, that would have been no bad thing. The days of the great Maseratis, the last of which was the awesome Bora V8, were long past. De Tomaso had attempted to turn the company into a sort of Italian BMW, but had instead produced a range of mediocre coupes, most of them under-powered, ill-handling, not especially well finished, inadequately reliable, and all of them grossly over-priced. They failed even on the first principle of the Italian high-performance car: they didn't even *look* exciting.

The abandonment of these cars and the ability to start the company from a blank sheet of paper would have been an exciting prospect, though whether Chrysler had the subtlety and understanding to match its resources to such a task we shall never know. Lamborghini became available, and that presented Chrysler with an entirely different set of interesting opportunities to exploit as well as problems to solve.

It took Chrysler quite a while to understand exactly what it had acquired. The chief difference between Maserati and Lamborghini was this: despite the various traumas, the comings and goings of different managements, the Lamborghini factory, thanks to a few key individuals, had retained its spirit. Engineering managers knew the direction in which they wanted the company to go. The workforce had regained its pride and had even acquired something approaching a sense of security, a rare commodity in industrial northern Italy.

Further than that, there was a superbly impressive product in the Countach 5000QV, in which a glossy image was fully matched by reality: the car was beautifully engineered and built to the highest standards by skilled craftsmen. It was regarded throughout the world as a pre-eminent 'macho' symbol of unashamed success. There was a long waiting list.

It is true that there were problems. The Jalpa, though basically a good car, had never fulfilled its promise – it hadn't quite become, as had been intended, the volume version of the Silhouette. Lamborghini has never yet succeeded in several attempts to produce an Italian 911, or even a Lamborghini to rival Ferrari's 308/328/348 Series.

But this in itself presented an attractive challenge. Should the Jalpa replacement simply be a re-skin (perhaps half the car's problem was its ungainly appearance, as its dimensions somehow give the appearance of being in conflict)? Should the excellent V8 (which at full throttle sounds very similar to the old three-litre Cosworth DFV engine) be retained and up-dated, or should a new engine (perhaps a fashionable V10) be designed? How many such cars could Lamborghini sell? More crucially, how many should they decide to build? (and how many Chrysler executives understand the subtle relationship between those two questions?).

What should be done about the LM? It was a monstrously impressive vehicle, it is true, but it hadn't attracted the military orders that had been hoped for, though it did achieve some success among customers wishing to out-do their Range Rover-owning neighbours, and was also popular in some Arab contries. Could a well-devised marketing exercise improve its sales? Could it be badged as a Chrysler? Should it be ruthlessly abandoned and concentration placed on car production?

As for the one really successful model in Lamborghini's range, the Countach, it had been developed about as far as a supercar conceived nearly twenty years previously could be. However, it was obvious that a replacement would soon be needed. Should it be constructed in the same way? Should it be designed by Gandini, or Giugiaro, or another Italian, or should the project be handed to Chrysler's design team in California? Should the concept of the car follow on directly from that of the Countach, or should it be a more modern, 'high-tech' type of supercar, with four-wheel drive, four-wheel

To most Countach fans, this is the definitive version: the
quattrovalvole, *without wings or side skirts. Gandini's single*
curve, stretching from nose to tail, is still evident here. It is one
of the boldest curves in the history of car design.

steering, anti-lock brakes and a wheelspin-limiting device? Again, should Lamborghini's engineers be fully in charge of the project, or should the control of the engineering development be in Detroit?

This leads us to the most crucial of all questions for Iacocca to consider: above all, how should the management structure of Lamborghini be changed to take account of the new ownership? Who should have responsibility for strategic decisions and who should control day-to-day management? These are the sorts of question which car manufacturers, large and small, must ask themselves every day, but it is more crucial for the answers to be correct in a smaller company because there is less room for error.

The relationship between a small, craft-based organisation and a large multinational company rarely proceeds without a few tears, tantrums and black eyes. It is essential that in the smaller company there should be strong-willed engineering managers, and in the larger one there should be executives with sufficient wisdom to stand back sometimes and allow decisions to be made which do not necessarily slot neatly into overall corporate policy.

When the Mimrans sold their interest in the company, Emile Novaro, who had been one of the company's top managers before he went with them to Lamborghini, stayed behind. He is now President and Managing Director, and he is the man who makes the key strategic decisions, after consultation (and occasionally confrontation) with the men from Detroit.

The chief representative of Chrysler at the Sant'Agata factory is Americanised Englishman Tony Richards. This is not exactly a duel, but if it were, Novaro's 'second' would be Venturelli, and Richards' would be Bob Smith.

That is the core of the current management team, but there are several other important people who should be mentioned, not least of whom is Ubaldo Sgarzi, now the Marketing Director. Others include Luigi Marmiroli and Daniele Audetto. Marmiroli

Giulio Alfieri, most famous for his work at Maserati, joined Lamborghini after failing to get on with volatile Alejandro de Tomaso. Alfieri's nephew, Giampaolo Dallara, had earlier been Lamborghini's chief engineer.

is a former member of the Alfa Romeo Grand Prix team, and was responsible for the technical development of the Anniversary model of the Countach, and is now fully in charge of the engineering of the Diablo and of other future Lamborghinis, including the Jalpa replacement. Daniele Audetto, a former Ferrari man who joined Lamborghini in the early 1980s, is the Managing Director of Lamborghini Engineering, and has responsibility for the Grand Prix engine programme and for the offshore powerboat team.

WHO RUNS LAMBORGHINI?

Lee Iacocca does not make direct decisions about the everyday work at Sant'Agata, but does seem to be concerned about the integrity of Lamborghini's reputation as a maker of fine Italian supercars. In the early months of 1989, Novaro had to go to Detroit to complain that the level of interference from Chrysler USA in the development of the Diablo, especially in the styling department, had become intolerable. Marmiroli and his team, and also Gandini, were continually fighting off attempts by Chrysler's design studios to take charge of the programme.

While the American engineers and designers were frantically trying to shape the exterior of the Diablo – and they almost succeeded – help requested by Marmiroli and other engineers on items like automatic gearboxes, active suspension, and so on, never materialised from Chrysler's technical centres. Apparently, some of the Americans were very keen on putting their signatures on the design of the body but not on the mechanical elements underneath it. They had failed to appreciate that the basis of Lamborghini's mystique is engineering excellence.

They are now behaving with more apparent sensitivity, partly under orders from above and partly as a result of hostile press reaction to projects like the Portofino, a ludicrous four-door styling exercise which was rushed out very quickly after Chrysler's acquisition of Lamborghini and displayed – much to the disgust of senior Lamborghini employees – at the 1987 Frankfurt Show. To rub salt into the wound, Iacocca himself appeared, rather in the style of a mafia boss, surrounded by a gang of bodyguards who cut a swathe through the crowded show hall.

Yet in the minds of some Chrysler people, the Portofino is still an 'interesting design for a possible Lamborghini', which is a damning comment upon their taste as well as an indication that their apprenticeship in high-quality, low-volume manufacturing may take longer than expected.

Novaro threatened to quit if the Italian engineers were not left alone. Iacocca promptly issued orders to stop the perpetual assault from the Detroit design people, stating that Lamborghini cars should be

Ferruccio Lamborghini with Chrysler boss Lee Iacocca at Salsomaggiore in 1988.

designed, shaped, engineered and produced by Lamborghini men.

After that, things were a lot better, which seems to suggest that Iacocca is serious in his respect for the reputation of Lamborghini; or perhaps it suggests that he respects a man like Novaro for being prepared to put his job on the line to stand up for an important principle.

Iacocca, whose salary is rumoured to be either ten or twenty million dollars per year (and one supposes that after the first ten, you stop counting), has acquired a house in Italy, at Grosseto, about 200 miles from the factory. He spends no more than a couple of weeks a year there. He ordered a Ferrari F40 for himself early in 1989, perhaps to evaluate the opposition, or perhaps more simply because he wanted a shiny new toy, or perhaps a shrewd investment.

And so, onwards into the future. Among many significant changes in the motor industry in the past few years has been the absorption of the bespoke car manufacturers into larger groups. Ferrari was the model for this, when it became a part of the Fiat empire. Lotus is owned by General Motors; Aston Martin and AC belong to Ford; Alpine is a division of Renault; Maserati is now part of Fiat, and Lamborghini has become part of Chrysler. Who knows what the long-term effects of all this will be? The retirement of Iacocca, which he recently announced and then immediately withdrew, may not in itself hold any great significance. After all, Bob Lutz, who is a great enthusiast whatever else he may be, will remain after Iacocca's departure.

Perhaps the crunch point will come when Mike Kimberley retires from Lotus, Victor Gauntlett from Aston Martin, and Emile Novaro from Lamborghini. Will their replacements be, respectively, a Lotus man, an Aston man and a Lamborghini man; or will they be grey men in suits from General Motors, Ford and Chrysler, who introduce themselves with the dread words 'I'm not just an accountant'?

SPECIFICATION
LP400

Engine

Location	Central
Cylinders	60deg V12, wet liners
Head material	Aluminium alloy
Block material	Aluminium alloy
Main bearings	7
Capacity, cc	3,929
Bore/stroke, mm	82/62
Compression ratio	10.5:1
Valve system	Twin camshafts per bank, driven by duplex chain, two valves per cylinder
Fuel system	Six twin-choke side-draught Weber 45 DCOE carburettors
Ignition system	Twin six-plug Marelli distributors
Cooling system	Pressurised, twin radiators vertically mounted either side of engine with crossover connection
Peak power, DIN bhp/rpm	375/8,000
Peak torque, DIN lb ft/rpm	266/5,500
Maximum rpm	8,000

Transmission

Location	Forward of engine
Type	Five-speed manual, limited-slip differential
Final drive ratio	4.091:1
Internal ratios and mph/1,00rpm	
5th	0.78:1/22.7
4th	0.99:1/17.5
3rd	1.31:1/13.5
2nd	1.77:1/10.1
1st	2.26 :1/8.0

Suspension

Front	Independent, by unequal-length wishbones, coil spring/damper units, anti-roll bar
Rear	Independent, by upper lateral links, lower reversed wishbones, upper and lower trailing arms, twin coil spring/damper units
Steering	Unassisted rack-and-pinion

Brakes

System	Girling vacuum-assisted, single servo, twin circuits split front/rear
Front	Ventilated discs, 10.5in (267mm) diameter
Rear	Ventilated discs, 10.5in (267mm) diameter

Wheels/tyres

Wheel type	Campagnolo cast magnesium alloy
Size, front/rear	14in×7.5JJ/14in×9JJ
Tyre type	Michelin XWX
Tyre size, front/rear	205–70 VR 14/215–70 VR 14

Body/chassis

Construction	Aluminium panels over round-section tubular spaceframe

Dimensions

Length, in/mm	163.0/4,140
Width, in/mm	74.4/1,890
Height, in/mm	42.1/1,069
Wheelbase, in/mm	96.5/2,451
Track, front:rear, in/mm	59.1:59.8/1,501:1,519
Fuel tank, gallons/litres	26.4/120
Kerb weight, cwt/kg	25.6/1,300.5

LP400S
As LP400 except:

Engine

Maximum power, DIN bhp/rpm	353/7,500
Maximum torque, DIN lb ft/rpm	267/5,500

Transmission

mph/1,000rpm

5th	22.3
4th	17.4
3rd	13.2
2nd	9.8
1st	7.7

Brakes

Front	Ventilated discs, 11.8in (300mm) diameter
Rear	Ventilated discs, 11.1in (282mm) diameter

Wheels/tyres

Wheel size, front/rear	15in×8.5J/15in×12J
Tyre type	Pirelli P7
Tyre size, front/rear	205–50 VR 15/345–35 VR 15

Dimensions

Kerb weight, cwt/kg	26.6/1,351

LP500S
As LP400S except:

Engine

Capacity, cc	4,754
Bore/stroke, mm	85.5/69
Compression ratio	9.2:1
Maximum power, DIN bhp/rpm	375/7,000
Maximum torque, DIN lb ft/rpm	302,/4,500

Transmission

Internal ratios and mph/1,000rpm

5th	0.707:1/24.4
4th	0.858:1/20.1
3rd	1.088:1/15.9
2nd	1.625:1/10.6
1st	2.232:1/7.7

Wheels/tyres

Size, front/rear	15in×8.5J/15in×12J
Tyre type	Pirelli P7
Tyre size, front/rear	225–50 VR 15/345–35 VR 15

Dimensions

Width, in/mm	78.7/1,999
Height, in/mm	42.1/1,069
Wheelbase, in/mm	96.5/2,451
Track, front: rear, in/mm	58.7:63.2/1,491:1,605

5000QV

As LP500S except:

Engine

Capacity, cc	5,167
Bore/stroke, mm	85.5/75
Compression ratio	9.5:1
Valve system	Four valves per cylinder
Fuel system	Six twin-choke down-draught Weber 44 DCNF carburettors
Ignition system	Marelli electronic
Peak power, bhp/rpm	455/7,000
Peak torque, lb ft/rpm	369/5,200

Brakes

Front	Ventilated discs, 11.8in (300mm) diameter
Rear	Ventilated discs, 11.2in (284mm) diameter

Dimensions

Width, in/mm	78.7/1,999
Wheelbase, in/mm	98.4/2,499
Track, front: rear, in/mm	60.5:63.2/1,537:1,605
Weight, cwt/kg	29.3/1,488

COUNTACH ANNIVERSARY

As 5000QV. The above figures refer to European versions of the Countach. A less powerful version is available for the USA, with three-way catalytic converter, and slightly different dimensions due to the addition of hideous bumpers to meet Federal regulations.

LAMBORGHINI DIABLO
(details in brackets for Diablo VT)

Engine

Cylinders	60deg V12, mid-mounted, longitudinal
Capacity, cc	5,709
Bore/stroke, mm	87/80
Compression ratio	10.0:1
Fuel system	L.I.E. sequential multi-point electronic injection; twin catalytic converters

Peak power, bhp/rpm	492/7,000
Peak torque, lb ft/rpm	428/5,200

Transmission

Type	Five-speed synchromesh, rear-wheel drive (four-wheel drive; front/rear torque split 80/20%)
Final drive ratio	2.41:1
Internal ratios and mph/1,000rpm	
5th	0.68:1/28.8
4th	0.88:1/22.3
3rd	1.12:1/17.5
2nd	1.52:1/12.9
1st	2.31 :1/8.5
Transfer ratio	1.59:1

Chassis

Type	Aluminium and composite body on square-tube steel spaceframe, with high-strength alloy survival cell, composite carbon fibre section.

Suspension

Front	Independent, by unequal-length double wishbones, coil springs, anti-roll bar; anti-dive/anti-squat geometry
Rear	Independent, by unequal-length double wishbones, coil springs, anti-roll bar
Steering	Unassisted rack-and-pinion

Brakes

System	Servo-assisted
Front	Ventilated discs, 13×1.26in (330×32mm)
Rear	Ventilated discs, 11.5×0.87in (284×22mm)

Wheels/tyres

Wheel type	Aluminium, three-piece
Size, front/rear	$8.5J \times 17$in (432mm)/$13J \times 17$in (432mm)
Tyre type	Pirelli P Zero
Front	245/40 ZR 17
Rear	335/35 ZR 17

Dimensions

Length, in/mm	175.5/4,458
Width, in/mm	80.3/2,040
Wheelbase, in/mm	104.3/2,649
Track, front:rear, in/mm	60.6:64.6/1,539:1,641
Fuel tank	22 gallons
Kerb weight, cwt/kg	32.5 (33.4)/1,651 (1,697)

Performance (factory figures)

Maximum speed	202 mph (325 kph)
0–60 mph (0–96.5 kph)	4.09sec
Standing km	20.7sec
Fuel consumption (composite)	14.9mpg

Lamborghini Clubs

Lamborghini Club UK
208 Latymer Court
Hammersmith Road
London W6 7JY
England

Lamborghini Owners Club
Jim Kaminski
P.O. Box 7214
St Petersburg
FL 33734
USA
Tel: (813) 823–3536

Nuova Lamborghini Owners Club
Jim Heady
4 Sol Brae Way
Orinda
CA 94563
USA
Tel: (415) 254–2107

Lamborghini Club Canada
Ken Browning
P.O. Box 543
Tilsonburg
Ontario
Canada N4G 4JI
Tel: (519) 842–9396

Index